annabel langbein
The Free Range Cook

Accompanying the TV Series

annabel langbein
The Free Range Cook

Contents

Welcome

Down at our little cabin in Central Otago at the foot of the Southern Alps, there's a rhythm to life that's so simple.

Most of what we eat comes from our gardens, the farm and our expeditions around the region to hunt, fish and gather. In our free time we head out to discover the region's riches and its artisan producers, picking cherries or walnuts and fishing out on the lake or over on the coast.

I cook on a double gas burner and chop wood to fuel the outdoor bread oven. When friends come over to share our gatherings we sit around the table for hours at a time enjoying informal meals and great conversations – eating and talking, laughing and sharing.

It's not about impressing people with gastronomic acrobatics, turning out complicated plates in the theatre of a restaurant. It's about having fun and celebrating what nature has so graciously provided for us.

There is little that is luxe about my cabin kitchen, or what we eat, in terms of either cost or effort. I am not talking about exotic or hard-to-find ingredients – rather the luxury of a perfectly ripe peach, fragrant and juicy, a glistening piece of fish just out of the water, or a beautifully aged piece of farm meat.

It is this simplicity that has inspired the idea of Free Range Cooking. It's about a pared-back approach to food and cooking that celebrates a spirit of resourcefulness, the pleasure of freshness, a sense of belonging in the community around you and the ability to live in the now, enjoying what is in season at its very best.

I could be doing this anywhere, because everywhere around the globe committed, clever people are devoting their lives to producing wonderful foods and wines. But Central Otago, with its majestic, raw beauty and bountiful riches from earth and water, has grabbed at my heart strings. When I am here I live a simple, good life.

Back in the city I can relive that life, using the farmers' markets to fine-tune my sense of what's in season, working my vege garden, getting to know my local providores, taking time for neighbours and friends, seeking in the city that simple rhythm of country life.

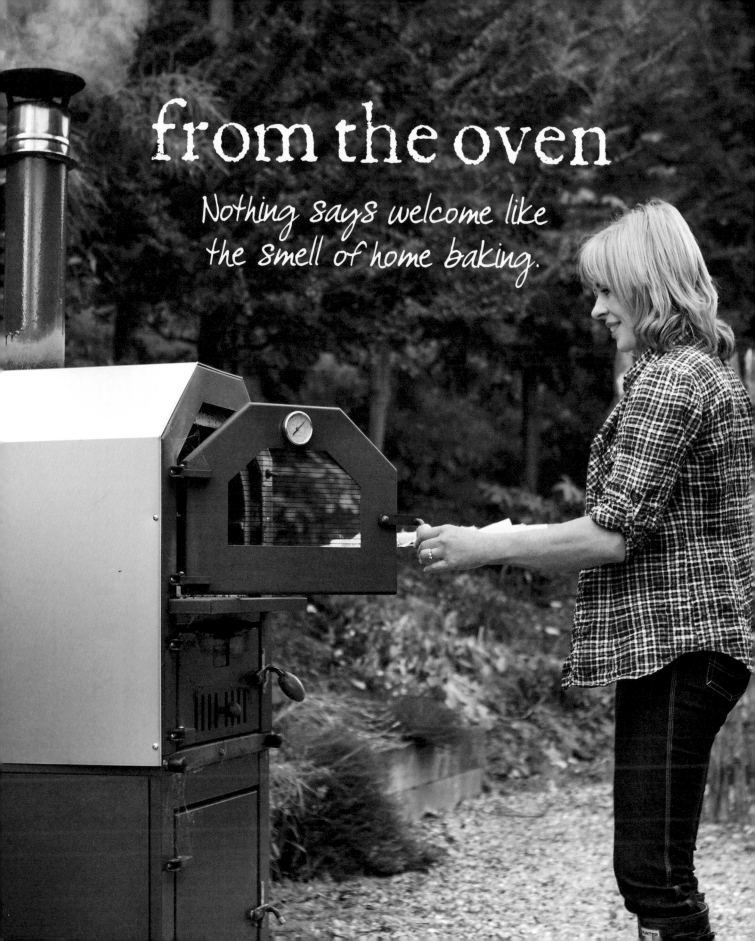

from the oven

Nothing says welcome like
the smell of home baking.

The aromas of nuts roasting, coffee brewing and bacon frying are guaranteed to whet our appetites. But it is the sweet smells of home baking that win us over every time, delivering that feel-good sense of comfort. Baking is a great place to start out in the kitchen – it's so easy to achieve success and create pleasure for everyone.

I have always loved to bake and in my early twenties I started my first business, making croissants in the then small seaside town of Buzios, just north of Rio. I still have the wonderful hand drawings my mother sent to me when I started out, which illustrate the process behind this layered yeast pastry.

I don't tend to make croissants these days but I still love to bake. On a rainy day when it is bleak outside there is nothing like the wafting smell of a cake in the oven to restore the spirits, and a loaf of bread straight out of the oven – with that irresistible nutty, grainy, yeasty aroma – offers pure solace.

The baking of my mother and paternal grandmother was a rhythm acquired by touch, taste and smell – a loaf was ready to come out of the oven when it sounded the hollow beat of a drum, and a cake would sing softly when it was perfectly cooked. In truth, baking is about chemistry and ratios, and while a seasoned cook may bake the lightest sponge or crispest pastry by touch over measure, a newcomer to the kitchen can achieve the same thrill of success simply by careful measurement and adherence to the recipe.

The alchemy of bread is gratifying well beyond the sum of its humble ingredients, offering in such a simple way a comforting sense of domesticity in our busy lives.

Sticky Buns

My children have been making these buns since they were about two. This is a large recipe, so half the recipe makes enough for 20 scrolls. The other half can be kept in the fridge for a couple of days or frozen for later use in other sweet breads including Festive Gubana and my Apricot and Custard Tricorns (see page 14).

Prep time	30 mins
	+ 1 hour
	20 mins rising
Cook time	12-15 mins
Makes	20

Sticky bun dough:
125g butter

2 cups milk

3 tsp dry yeast granules

¾ cup sugar

6 cups high-grade flour

1 tsp salt

To fill:
6 tbsp butter, softened but not melted

½ cup sugar

1 tbsp cinnamon

Optional glaze:
¼ cup sugar

3 tbsp water

To dust:
icing sugar

Place the butter in a small pot and heat gently until melted. Remove from the heat and add the milk. The mixture should be at blood temperature before you sprinkle the yeast and sugar over the top. Stir for a minute or two until the yeast is absorbed.

Mix flour and salt together in a large bowl. Add the milk mixture and stir until just combined. Tip the dough onto a lightly floured surface and knead until smooth and silky – about 60-100 kneading strokes. Place the dough in a large, lightly oiled container, cover with a clean cloth and leave to rise in a warm place until it has almost doubled in size – about 1 hour.

When risen, divide the dough in half and refrigerate or freeze one half for later use. Roll the other half out to a 60 x 30cm rectangle on a lightly floured board. To fill, brush the rolled dough liberally with the softened butter. Mix together the sugar and cinnamon and sprinkle over the top of the butter. Roll the dough up tightly along the longest edge into a cylinder shape. Cut into slices about 4cm wide. You should have about 20 scrolls.

Line the base of a 28-30cm round cake tin with baking paper. Arrange the scrolls in the lined cake tin, allowing 1-2cm between them. Cover with a clean tea towel and leave to rise in a warm place (not hot or the butter will melt) for 20 minutes.

While the scrolls are rising, preheat the oven to 220°C. Bake scrolls for 12-15 minutes until golden and cooked through.

To glaze the scrolls, heat the sugar and water in a small pot until the sugar is dissolved. Boil for 5 minutes. Brush the scrolls with hot syrup as they emerge from the oven or dust with icing sugar.

To make in a bread maker: Place all the ingredients except the filling and glaze in a bread maker and put on dough mode. Once the dough has risen, divide it in half, roll out and continue as above.

Festive Gubana

My Sticky Bun Dough (see page 13) is a versatile starting point for a variety of baked treats like this gubana, a rolled sweet bread that is traditionally eaten at Easter, Christmas and weddings in parts of northern Italy.

Prep time	10 mins + rising
Cook time	30 mins
Serves	6-8

½ recipe Sticky Bun Dough
(see page 13)

1½ cups sweet fruit mince

½ cup chocolate chips

To dust:
icing sugar

Preheat oven to 180°C. Line a 26-28cm round cake tin with baking paper.

Roll dough out to a thickness of about 1cm to form a 60 x 30cm rectangle. Spread the fruit mince over the dough, leaving a 2cm border. Sprinkle chocolate chips over the top. Roll dough up tightly along the longest edge to create a long cylinder shape. Form the dough cylinder into a tight spiral and place it in the lined cake tin.

Cover with a clean teatowel and leave to rise in a warm place for 45 minutes until nearly doubled in size. Bake for 30 minutes until golden and cooked through. Dust with icing sugar to serve.

Apricot and Custard Tricorns

Preheat oven to 220°C and line a baking tray with baking paper. Roll out half a quantity of Sticky Bun Dough (see page 13) to a thickness of 1cm. Cut into 10-12 triangles. Top each triangle with a spoonful of custard (1 cup in total) and half a cooked or canned apricot, cut side down. Melt ¼ cup apricot jam and brush it over the tops of the apricots. Pinch the corners of the dough to partially enclose the custard and apricot. Place on the lined baking tray and allow to rise for 20 minutes before baking for about 30 minutes until golden. Makes 10-12.

Sweet Apricot Breakfast Bread

Add sugar to my basic Crusty Flat Bread recipe (see page 18) and it's transformed into a tender sweet bread that's great for breakfast or a morning tea treat. If you don't have dried apricots it can be made with other fruit. Try pairing halved fresh grapes or figs with fennel seeds or halved plums with a dusting of star anise.

Prep time	20 mins +
	10 mins rising
Cook time	25-30 mins
Serves	6-8

½ recipe Crusty Flat Bread Dough (see page 18) made with just 1 tsp salt and ½ cup white sugar added to flour

a little water

½ cup brown sugar

12 dried apricots

1 tsp mixed spice

To dust:
icing sugar

Follow the instructions for Crusty Flat Bread up to the point where the dough is pressed out on a lined tray into an oval shape about 25 x 20cm.

Place a baking stone on the centre shelf of the oven and preheat oven to 220°C. Let the bread rise for about 10 minutes, then brush lightly with water (this makes the sugar melt) and sprinkle with brown sugar. Press the dried apricots into the dough, creating dimples as you go. Sprinkle with mixed spice.

Slide the baking paper with the dough on it onto the preheated baking stone. Bake for 15 minutes, then reduce the heat to 180°C and cook for a further 10-15 minutes until the bread is golden and cooked through.

Remove bread from oven, allow it to cool for a few minutes and then dust with icing sugar. Cut into pieces with a sharp knife and serve. This is best eaten the day it is made.

Crusty Flat Bread

This is a wonderfully supple focaccia dough that makes enough for two large loaves. You can freeze the excess or use it to make Parmesan and Basil Dimples (see page 20), Cheese and Ham Twists (see page 25) and Vegetable Calzone (see page 26). I use leftover mashed potato but if you don't have any in the fridge, boil potatoes until tender, mash them and allow to cool before adding to the recipe. The wetter the dough is, the lighter the finished result will be so don't be tempted to keep adding flour.

Prep time	20 mins + 3 hours rising or 12 hours in the fridge
Cook time	25 mins
Makes	2 large loaves

Crusty flat bread dough:

1½ cups warm (not hot) water

1½ tsp dry yeast granules

1 packed cup cooked mashed potato

¼ cup extra virgin olive oil

4½ cups high-grade or baker's flour, plus extra for kneading

2 tsp salt

Topping:

1-2 tbsp extra virgin olive oil

2 tsp fresh rosemary leaves

½ tsp sea salt

Place warm water in a large mixing bowl (a bread maker or electric mixer with a dough blade is ideal if you have one). Sprinkle yeast over the water and allow to stand for 2 minutes. Mix in the mashed potato and the ¼ cup olive oil. Stir in the flour and salt and mix until the dough just starts to come away from the sides of the bowl.

Turn the dough onto a lightly floured board and using lightly oiled hands knead about 30 times (or for 3-4 minutes on the dough cycle of a bread maker). Place the dough into a lightly oiled bowl. Cover with muslin or a teatowel and leave to rise in a warm place for 3-4 hours or until it has doubled in bulk. You can also leave it in the fridge, covered, to rise slowly overnight.

When you're ready to cook your bread, place a baking stone on the centre shelf of the oven and preheat oven to 220°C. Turn the risen dough onto a lightly floured board, divide in half and shape each half into a ball. Roughly flatten one ball onto a tray lined with baking paper, pressing the dough out to an oval shape about 25 x 20cm. Use your fingertips to press dimples into the top of the loaf, then drizzle with olive oil and sprinkle with rosemary and sea salt.

Slide the baking paper with the dough on it off the tray and onto the preheated baking stone. Bake for about 25 minutes until golden. When cooked the bread will sound hollow when you tap it. Remove from the oven and allow to cool on the baking stone for a few minutes, then transfer to a rack to cool.

Repeat with the other ball of dough. If you want to save the second ball of dough to use later, place it in a lightly oiled bowl, cover with a clean cloth and place in the fridge for up to 48 hours. It also freezes well. Thaw before pressing out and baking.

Parmesan and Basil Dimples

My friend Paula's mother, Marili Mustilli, is a wonderful cook. At the family trattoria in Italy she serves these pillow-like breads as just one of several impressive antipasti. They are part of a vast repertoire of Puglese flavours handed down in her family. Best of all, they can be made with my Crusty Flat Bread Dough (see page 18).

Prep time	10-15 mins
Cook time	20-25 mins
Makes	24-30

½ recipe Crusty Flat Bread Dough (see page 18)

To fry:
rice bran oil

To serve:
1 cup Tomato Passata (see page 64)
or tomato pasta sauce

⅓ cup grated mozzarella or grated parmesan cheese

24-30 small basil leaves

Prepare the dough by following the instructions for Crusty Flat Bread up to the point where the dough has risen and doubled in bulk.

Sprinkle a little flour on a board or bench then roll the dough into a long sausage. Cut the dough into 24-30 evenly sized pieces. Roll each piece into a ball then flatten with the floured palm of your hand. Allow the dough to rest for a few minutes then roll each piece out so it is about 1cm thick. Press your thumb into the centre of each rolled round to create a light dimple.

Pour the cooking oil into a medium pot to a depth of about 2cm. Heat the oil over a medium heat until it is hot enough that a small piece of dough starts to sizzle vigorously as soon as it is added. Fry the dough rounds 3 or 4 at a time until they are golden on the bottom, then flip to cook the other side. Remove from the oil and drain on paper towels. Serve topped with fresh Tomato Passata or tomato pasta sauce, mozzarella or parmesan and basil leaves.

If desired these can be heated under the grill before garnishing with the basil leaves. You can also make them ahead of time and reheat in a hot oven for a few minutes before topping with Tomato Passata or tomato pasta sauce, parmesan and basil and serving.

Gathering wood, lighting
a fire and baking bread
or buns — simple rituals
that deliver big rewards.

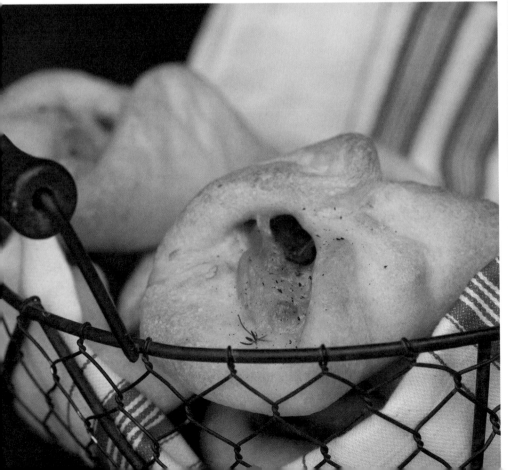

Crusty Olive, Tomato and Caper Flat Bread

This loaf is another fantastic way to use my Crusty Flat Bread Dough (see page 18). It's perfect for a picnic. Take along a wedge of cheese and you have a simple meal.

Prep time	15 mins +
	30 mins rising
Cook time	20 mins
Makes	1 large loaf

½ recipe Crusty Flat Bread Dough (see page 18)

½ cup pitted black olives

2 large tomatoes

1 tbsp capers

2 tbsp extra virgin olive oil

1 tbsp fresh oregano, chopped

1 tsp fresh rosemary, chopped

Prepare the bread dough by following the instructions for Crusty Flat Bread up to the point where the dough is turned onto a tray lined with baking paper. Form it into a flat oblong shape and leave in a warm place for 30 minutes to rise.

When you're ready to cook your bread, place a baking stone on the centre shelf of the oven and preheat oven to 220°C.

Chop olives, core and finely dice tomatoes and combine with the rest of the ingredients in a bowl. Scatter over the top of the risen loaf. Slide the baking paper with the dough on it off the tray and onto the preheated baking stone. Bake for about 20 minutes until the bread is golden and sounds hollow when tapped. Allow to cool on the baking stone for a few minutes then transfer to a rack to cool.

Cheese and Ham Twists

Pop these into lunchboxes frozen and they'll be thawed by morning tea time!

Prep time	10 mins
Cook time	15-20 mins
Serves	8

½ recipe Crusty Flat Bread Dough (see page 18)

4 slices ham, cut in half, and/or 8 slices tomato or salami

1 cup mozzarella, grated

salt and ground black pepper

To sprinkle:
dried oregano

Prepare the bread dough by following the instructions for Crusty Flat Bread up to the point where the dough has doubled in bulk. Preheat oven to 220°C. Cut the dough into 8 evenly sized pieces and on a lightly floured board roll each piece into a rough square about 12 x 12cm. For easy handling, place the squares of dough onto an oven tray lined with baking paper.

Place ham, tomato or salami on top of the dough squares. Sprinkle with mozzarella cheese and season to taste. To create the twists, fold two opposite corners of dough over to the centre, overlapping them slightly and pinching together to secure. Sprinkle with oregano.

Bake the twists for 15-20 minutes until they are golden and the dough is cooked and crisp. Serve hot or at room temperature.

Vegetable Calzone

Calzone is a marvellous portable pie made by sandwiching a flavoursome vegetable filling inside dough and then baking it. Here I've created a delicious variation using my Crusty Flat Bread Dough (see page 18) with tasty vegetables and cheese baked on top.

Prep time | 15 mins
Cook time | 65 mins
Makes | 1 large pie
Serves | 4

½ recipe Crusty Flat Bread Dough (see page 18)

2 tbsp extra virgin olive oil

2 red or yellow capsicums, white membranes and seeds discarded, flesh sliced into thin strips

2 cloves garlic, minced

1 tbsp capers

1 tsp fresh rosemary, chopped or ½ tsp dried rosemary

400g can artichokes, drained and roughly chopped

salt and ground black pepper

100g mozzarella cheese, thinly sliced

20 fresh basil leaves, shredded finely

Prepare the bread dough by following the instructions for Crusty Flat Bread up to the point where the dough has risen and doubled in bulk. While it is rising, prepare the filling. Heat the oil in a frypan then add the capsicums, garlic, capers and rosemary. Cover and cook over a gentle heat for 15 minutes. Mix in the artichokes and season to taste. Cool.

Preheat oven to 200°C. Turn the dough out onto an oiled baking tray and press it out into a circle shape about 30cm in diameter. Spread with filling and top with cheese, leaving a border of clean dough about 6cm wide around the outside.

Bake for 10 minutes then reduce the heat to 180°C and cook for another 40 minutes. Remove from the oven, top with the basil leaves and serve warm or at room temperature.

Busy People's Bread

A lot of people are put off making bread because they think of it as a time consuming exercise. If you fall into that camp then give this super quick bread a whirl. It's a simple one mix dough that you don't have to let rise because it rises in the oven during the first stage of low temperature cooking.

Prep time	10 mins
Cook time	50-60 mins
Makes	2 loaves

2 cups boiling water

4 tsp honey

2 cups cold water

7 tsp dry yeast granules

2¾ cups high-grade white flour

2¾ cups wholemeal flour

3 tsp salt

2 cups sunflower seeds

4 tbsp pumpkin seeds

Preheat oven to just 80°C and grease and line two 25 x 10cm loaf tins with baking paper.

In a large bowl, mix the boiling water with the honey to dissolve. Add the cold water and yeast and put to one side for 10 minutes.

Whisk the yeast mixture then add white and wholemeal flour, salt and sunflower seeds and mix with a large spoon until evenly combined. (The mixture will be a very loose, wet batter.)

Divide mixture between prepared loaf tins, spread evenly and flatten the top. Sprinkle 2 tbsp pumpkin seeds over the top of each loaf and, run a sharp knife through the top of each loaf in at least 3 or 4 places so it rises evenly without splitting.

Bake for 20 minutes at 80°C and then turn up the oven to 210°C and bake for a further 30-40 minutes. When cooked, the loaves will sound hollow when tapped. Turn out of the tins while still hot and leave to cool. This bread stays fresh for several days and toasts well.

Open Sandwiches

Liberally coat 4 slices of Busy People's Bread (see above) with 4 tbsp Horseradish Cream (see page 181). Top each slice with a few sprigs of land cress or some rocket leaves, 2 slices of cold smoked salmon and a sprinkle of very thinly sliced red onion. Garnish with fresh chervil or Italian parsley.

Sesame and Oregano Lavosh

Lavosh is a thin, crunchy Middle Eastern bread that's delicious as a picnic snack or served as a pre-dinner nibble with blue cheese and dried fruit. In this recipe I flavour it with sesame and oregano, but you could also use fennel seeds, parmesan or chillies. The wholemeal flour adds texture and makes it a healthy oven-baked snack. Cut any shapes you like – as long as the dough is very thin you'll get a fabulous crisp bread.

Prep time	15 mins
Cook time	15-18 mins
Makes	approx 40

1 cup plain flour

⅓ cup wholemeal flour

2 tbsp each black and white sesame seeds
or 4 tbsp just one kind

1 tbsp finely chopped fresh oregano
or 1 tsp dried oregano

1 tsp salt

¼ cup extra virgin olive oil

1 tsp sesame oil

½ cup water

To finish:
extra virgin olive oil

flaky sea salt

Preheat oven to 165°C and line an oven tray with baking paper.
In a mixing bowl stir together the flours, sesame seeds, oregano and salt. Mix the oils and water together and add to the dry ingredients, stirring to form a soft, pliable dough.

Divide the dough into 4 pieces and roll each out on a lightly floured board as thinly as possible. Each piece of dough should yield a rectangle about 34 x 16cm. Cut each rectangle into strips measuring about 4 x 17cm and roll again. They need to be virtually see-through.

Carefully transfer strips to a baking tray, brush lightly with oil and sprinkle with flaky salt. Bake until crisp and pale golden – about 15-18 minutes. Allow to cool fully then store in an airtight container.

Watch Annabel make this recipe at thefreerangecook.com

Lamb, Rosemary and Apple Sausage Rolls

The inclusion of apple makes these homemade sausage rolls light and moist. You could add different flavourings to the base mixture of meat, apple, egg and onion – make a Greek version with olives, garlic, rosemary and feta or an Italian option with basil, sundried tomatoes and garlic. If you can't find good quality sausage meat, cut open the skins of your favourite sausages and squeeze out the meat.

Prep time	10 mins
Cook time	30-35 mins
Serves	6
Makes	6 big rolls or 12-18 small rolls

400g lean lamb mince

250g coarse sausage meat such as pork or beef

1 apple, unpeeled, coarsely grated

2 eggs (1 separated)

1 small onion, peeled and coarsely grated

1 clove garlic, crushed

2 tbsp chopped parsley

½ tsp chopped rosemary

3 finely chopped sage leaves

1 tsp fruit chutney or tomato sauce

1 tsp salt

ground black pepper

pinch chilli flakes

2 sheets of flaky pastry

Preheat oven to 200°C and line an oven tray with baking paper.

Place the mince and sausage meat in a large bowl with the grated apple, whole egg and egg white, onion, garlic, herbs, chutney or tomato sauce, salt, pepper and chilli. Mix with a large spoon until evenly incorporated.

Place the two pastry sheets on a work surface. Place half the meat mixture on each pastry sheet, forming a mound the length of the pastry about 6cm in from one edge.

Roll up the pastry to fully enclose the filling. Cut each roll into 3 slices (or up to 6 slices if you want small sausage rolls), and place on the lined baking tray seam side down.

Use a sharp knife to slash 2 or 3 lines across the top of each sausage roll to allow the steam to escape. Make a glaze by mixing the egg yolk with 1 tbsp water. Brush over the pastry.

Bake for 30-35 minutes or until golden brown. Check in the last 10 minutes of cooking and if any liquids have come out of the rolls, soak them up with a paper towel so the pastry stays crisp.

Quesadillas

Quesadillas (pronounced kay-sa-dee-ya) are toasted sandwiches made with flour or corn tortillas. They are the Mexican equivalent of pizza and just as versatile. With the addition of adventurous fillings such as olive paste or pesto, spicy sausage or parma ham and good cheese they make a great snack or supper, or an accompaniment to soups or salads.

Prep time	5 mins
Cook time	2-5 mins in pan or 8-10 mins in oven
Serves	4

2 fresh flour tortillas

slices of cheese, to cover

sliced tomatoes, to cover

5-6 basil leaves
or 1 tsp basil pesto

salt and pepper

If using a frypan to cook your quesadillas, first heat up the pan. Once it is hot, place a tortilla in the pan. Cover with filling ingredients, then place another tortilla on top. Cook until the bottom of the tortilla starts to turn golden, then carefully flip over and cook the other side until golden. You can also use just 1 tortilla, fill it only to the halfway line and then fold it over.

If you are cooking a lot of quesadillas, it's easiest to do it in the oven. Preheat oven to 200°C. Sandwich the filling ingredients between 2 whole tortillas, place quesadillas on a baking tray, weight with another baking tray on top and bake for 8-10 minutes until golden. Cut into wedges to serve.

Mushroom Bruschetta

This fantastic appetiser or snack is as simple as tossing mushrooms in Roasted Garlic Aioli (see page 56), piling them onto bread and baking the whole caboodle until crispy.

Prep time	5 mins
Cook time	20-30 mins
Makes	6 slices

200g mushrooms, thinly sliced

3-4 tbsp Roasted Garlic Aioli
(see page 56)
or good quality mayonnaise

salt and ground black pepper

6 large slices sourdough
or 18 small rounds French stick

Preheat oven to 180°C. Mix the mushroom slices with just enough Roasted Garlic Aioli or mayonnaise to coat them and season with salt and pepper. Pile the mushrooms onto the slices of bread and bake for 20-30 minutes until the bread is crunchy on the base and the mushrooms are golden. Serve hot.

There's a wonderful sense of getting something for nothing when you forage for wild food.

Caramelised Onion and Feta Tart

People often avoid making flaky pastry because they think it will be too hard, but my homemade version is super easy and delivers a buttery, melt-in-the-mouth result you'll never taste in store bought pastry. The trick is to not overwork the dough, or it will be tough. This pastry can be frozen and can also be made in a food processor. If that still sounds too hard, use 500g commercial flaky pastry instead.

Prep time	20 mins +
	10 mins chilling
Cook time	50-55 mins
Serves	8

Flaky pastry:

2 cups high-grade flour

1 tsp salt

1 tsp baking powder

220g frozen butter, grated

¼ cup iced water

Filling:

3 cups Caramelised Onions (see page 86)

150g sheep feta or other feta, grated or crumbled

2 tsp fresh thyme leaves or 1 tsp dried thyme

Start by making the pastry. Combine the flour, salt and baking powder in a bowl. Mix in the grated butter and work a little with your fingertips until the mixture resembles rough crumbs. Then add the water, mixing just until a soft dough is formed.

Place a large sheet of baking paper on the bench and tip the dough onto this, pressing it together with your hands. Place another sheet of baking paper over the dough and roll the pastry out with a rolling pin into a circle approx 35cm in diameter.

Transfer to a baking tray and chill for at least 10 minutes or until ready to assemble. Chilling pastry prevents shrinking during cooking.

Preheat oven to 200°C. Take your pastry base from the fridge and remove the top layer of baking paper. Spread the Caramelised Onions over the top of the pastry, leaving a 4cm border around the edge. Crumble the feta over the top and sprinkle with thyme.

Fold the pastry edges in towards the centre to partially enclose the filling, then pleat in little folds to make a pastry border. Bake for 15 minutes then reduce heat to 180°C for a further 35-40 minutes until golden and crisp. Serve hot accompanied by green salad.

Bacon and Egg Pie

If you're looking for love, you have to make this pie! On the strength of this pie, my husband proposed to me – it really is that good. It's perfect for a picnic or weekend lunch.

Prep time   10 mins
Cook time   45-55 mins
Serves   6-8

3 sheets (450g) ready-rolled savoury shortcrust pastry

250g streaky bacon, cut into 2cm pieces

2 medium potatoes, peeled, cooked and thinly sliced

3 tbsp soft herbs such as parsley, basil, chives or spring onion tops, chopped

14 eggs

¾ cup milk

·1 tsp salt

ground black pepper

Preheat oven to 200°C. Place a flat baking tray in the oven to heat – the pie will sit on this and the heat will help it to crisp.

Cut a piece of baking paper to fit a 40 x 30cm baking dish or roasting pan. It should cover the base and reach about 3-4cm up the sides. Remove the baking paper from the baking dish or roasting pan and lay it flat on your bench. Dust it with a little flour and lay 2 pastry sheets on top. Join the pastry sheets by pressing them together firmly with a small overlap. Roll out the pastry to cover the paper. Lift the paper with the pastry and lay it into the baking dish or roasting pan (it will reach 3-4cm up the sides).

Sprinkle the bacon over the pastry. Top with the sliced potato and sprinkle with the herbs. Break 8 whole eggs over the top.

In a mixing bowl, lightly whisk the remaining 6 eggs with the milk, salt and pepper. Pour this evenly over the whole eggs.

Roll out the remaining sheet of pastry very thinly and cut it into narrow strips. Arrange the strips in a lattice pattern on top of the pie, trimming off any excess.

Place the prepared pie on top of the heated baking tray and bake for 12-15 minutes until the pastry is starting to puff and turn golden. Reduce the heat to 180°C and bake until the pastry is golden and cooked through on the base – about a further 35-40 minutes.

Serve warm or at room temperature with a salad and pickles or chutney. It will keep in a covered container in the fridge for 2-3 days.

Watch Annabel make this recipe at thefreerangecook.com

Confidence is probably the key to enjoying cooking. If you're relaxed everyone else will be too.

from the garden

When you start with really
fresh ingredients it's easy
to be a great cook.

The fresher your ingredients, the less work for you in the kitchen. Slice tomatoes and toss with oil and herbs, boil corn and toss with butter, or scrub potatoes and toss with rosemary, salt and oil, then roast till golden and crispy. With nature on your side it's easy to be a great cook and enjoy delicious meals at the drop of a hat.

It's not until you've tasted a juicy tomato vine-ripened by the sun, or a crisply sweet carrot just pulled from the earth, that you realise what you have been missing. Flavour goes a long way to explain the phenomenal popularity of farmers' markets and backyard vegetable gardens. In the freshly picked harvests of local growers and our own gardens, we discover old and lesser known varieties grown because they taste good, not because they suit the long life requirements of a supermarket supply chain. The fluorescent atmosphere of a supermarket may make everything look good, but looks don't necessarily equate to flavour or succulence.

Beyond the opportunity for family farms and artisan producers to sell locally grown, caught, foraged, baked and preserved products, farmers' markets create community – something fast disappearing from our lives as people get busier and the big chains bump out the old-timer providores.

Each week at the markets, the same friendly faces greet and cajole. Before you know it you're trying something new, tempted by an artisan spread, sweet baby peas or, in the case of New York's famous Union Square market, small, sweet green shisito chillies fried in oil. They are every reason to visit that particular market through late summer and autumn. Through the flavours of other cultures we expand our culinary horizons and bring new tastes and ingredients into our own kitchens.

A wander around my garden invariably provides the inspiration for our evening meals. Last night I picked two fat bulbs of fennel and some silverbeet. I sliced up the fennel and some red onions, cooking them in a little oil with a couple of diced rashers of bacon, fresh thyme and bay leaves for flavour. This went into a baking dish with pieces of browned chicken on top and a little stock. Then the whole lot went into the oven to bake for 40 minutes. The silverbeet was cooked with a dash of water and a slug of olive oil. Served with a side of wet polenta, it was a simple meal that had everyone licking their lips.

Following the idea of baking chicken on a bed of vegetables, you could change the fennel for leeks, or use a mix of zucchini, onions, peppers and tomatoes, or sliced potatoes, garlic, olives and rosemary. Each tangent will create something a little different, but no less delicious. Such is the hallmark of home cooking – a resourceful, creative approach that relies on freshness, drawing on flavours and ingredients as the seasons dictate.

The mirror that for the most part exists between our appetites and the offerings of the season makes it easy to cook in sync with nature's harvests.

In winter we stave off the cold with rib-sticking stews, soups and big bowls of mash – all those dishes that root vegetables and winter greens deliver so well. By the time spring comes around we crave the fresh, soft tastes of the green shoots and leaves that emerge as the earth starts to warm. In the dog days of summer, raw tastes abound, satisfying our desire for simple one-toss meals and time out from the kitchen. As the crisp days of autumn arrive, a deluge of harvests find their way into trays of slow-roasted vegetables, rich sauces and satisfying vegetable stews – the perfect segue for appetites reviving after a summer's heat.

Roasted Beet and Rocket Salad

Caramelised beets, creamy feta and almonds are a great combination in this simple salad.

Prep time	10 mins
Cook time	45 mins
Serves	6

4-5 medium (400-500g)
beetroot, peeled
and cut into 2cm wedges

2 tbsp extra virgin olive oil

1 tbsp brown sugar

1 tbsp balsamic vinegar

salt and ground black pepper

8 small handfuls (200g)
rocket leaves

1 handful (25g) baby beet
leaves (optional)

juice of 1 lemon

2 tbsp extra virgin olive oil

1 cup roasted almonds

120g feta cheese, crumbled
or grated

Preheat oven to 180°C. Place the beetroot wedges in a large roasting dish lined with baking paper and mix through the first measure of oil, sugar, vinegar and salt and pepper. Spread out into a single layer.

Roast for 40-45 minutes until tender and just starting to shrivel. Allow beets to cool in the roasting dish.

Toss rocket leaves and baby beet leaves, if using, with the lemon juice and the second measure of olive oil and divide between 6 serving plates. Divide cooled roasted beetroot over the top and scatter with almonds and feta to serve.

Learning the taste of something just picked allows you to start imagining other flavours that might work with it and opens the door to your own cooking style.

Leafy Salad with Walnuts and Blue Cheese

This salad makes a great side dish at dinner time or a healthy light lunch on its own. Dress the salad at the last minute or it will go soggy.

Prep time	15 mins
Cook time	10 mins
Serves	5-6

½ cup walnuts

6 handfuls (150g) mixed salad greens, washed and dried

60-80g blue cheese, crumbled

¼ cup Dijon Mustard Vinaigrette (see below)

Preheat the oven to 180°C. Place the walnuts in an oven dish and roast them for 10 minutes until toasted but not blackened. Put the salad greens in a large serving bowl and sprinkle with the toasted walnuts and the blue cheese. Just before serving, drizzle with Dijon Mustard Vinaigrette and toss to combine.

Leafy Salad with Orange and Avocado

Prepare salad as above, replacing walnuts and blue cheese with 3 oranges cut into segments and 1 sliced avocado.

Leafy Salad with Feta and Cherry Tomatoes

Prepare salad as above, replacing walnuts and blue cheese with 12 cherry tomatoes and 150g crumbled feta.

Dijon Mustard Vinaigrette

Everyone has their own favourite dressing for everyday use. This is mine. In a jar combine ⅔ cup extra virgin olive oil, 3 tsp lemon juice, 1 tbsp wine vinegar, 1 tsp Dijon mustard, 1 tsp sugar, ½ tsp salt, ground pepper and 1 clove crushed garlic. Shake well to emulsify. Taste and adjust ingredients to your own taste. If it's too acidic add more oil, too sour add more sugar – you're aiming for a pleasant balance of flavours. Keeps in the fridge for weeks.

Green Bean and Peanut Noodles

Noodles are a fast cooking side dish for any Asian meal. Rice stick noodles require almost no cooking and are an inexpensive and useful pantry staple.

Prep time	10 mins
Cook time	5 mins
Serves	6

6 handfuls (300g) green beans, stalk ends trimmed

250g rice stick noodles

½ cup roasted peanuts, roughly chopped

3 tbsp roughly chopped coriander

1 tbsp sesame seeds, toasted

2 cups bean sprouts

½ tsp salt

ground black pepper

For the dressing:
1 tbsp sesame oil

2 tbsp grapeseed or other neutral oil

2 tsp fish sauce

To serve:
lime wedges

Cut the beans in half and boil them in salted water for 3 minutes. Refresh in cold water to retain their crunch and bright green colour.

Drop the rice noodles into a large pot of boiling water. Remove the pot from the heat immediately and allow to stand and cool for 10 minutes or longer. Drain the noodles then rinse in cold water.

Put the beans and cooked, drained noodles in a large serving bowl with the roasted peanuts, coriander, sesame seeds and bean sprouts.

Make the dressing by putting the sesame oil, neutral oil and fish sauce in a jar and shaking to combine. Toss the dressing through the noodles and season to taste with salt and pepper.

Serve as a salad at room temperature or toss in a hot pan for 2-3 minutes for a stir fry side dish to serve with meats. Garnish with lime wedges to serve.

Creating a vegetable garden

There is something deeply satisfying about growing your own vegetables. Beyond the gratification of having produced something exquisitely fresh for your own dinner, a vegetable garden offers a wonderfully grounding connection to nature and a simple understanding of its rhythms.

The cycle of life is revealed in a plant, be it lettuce or broccoli – the tiny seed germinates, grows into leafy abundance, produces flowers, forms seeds and, with its genetic code fulfilled, finally dies. The seeds will rest in the ground until either temperature or light kick off the process all over again, producing the next year's harvests. And so it goes on.

Even if it's just a pot of basil growing on the kitchen windowsill, its leaves to be made into pesto, tossed through pasta or stirred into a sauce, there's a sense of participation that connects you to the plate in a simple yet fundamental way.

Whenever I get the chance I am out in the garden, turning the earth, planting seeds, harvesting or seed saving. People who don't garden bemoan the hard work, incredulous that such a messy, physically demanding activity could be so pleasurable.

When we started planning for the television series that accompanies this book, my husband Ted and I decided to plant a big garden on a terrace in the windswept paddock that overlooks the lake at our Wanaka hideaway.

Our first germinations were demolished by rabbits. Up went a ring fence. Then we battled the wind, fierce nor'westers ripping leaves and turning the garden to brittle dryness. Up went a wall of hay bales.

Some things prospered, others, like the runner beans, pretty much failed. We were too late getting in most of the corn, and the tomatoes struggled in the coldest summer for decades.

But for all the vagaries of nature, this new garden has given us a tremendous sense of achievement and pleasure. From bare earth, in just a few months we have picked a mountain of wonderful harvests. Beyond this, in the interspersed plantings of red cabbages, blue-grey Tuscan cabbages, artichokes, salvia, dahlias and beets, it is a beautiful place to just stop and breathe.

Pear, Walnut and Haloumi Salad

Peppery watercress, creamy haloumi cheese and sweet pear harmonise beautifully in this lovely salad. I prefer to use Cypriot-style haloumi as it holds its shape nicely.

Prep time   15 mins
Cook time   10-20 mins
Serves   6 as a starter

4 tbsp neutral oil
(eg grapeseed)

1 cup fresh walnut pieces

2 just ripe pears

juice of ½ lemon

250g haloumi, thinly sliced

6 handfuls (150g) fresh
watercress sprigs
or baby spinach leaves

2 avocados, cut into chunks
(optional)

salt and ground black pepper

Heat 3 tbsp of the neutral oil in a frypan and fry the walnuts over a medium heat until lightly browned – about 2-3 minutes. Lift out of the oil with a slotted spoon and drain on a paper towel. Reserve the oil to dress the salad. Alternatively, roast them dry on an oven tray at 180°C for 12-15 minutes.

Halve and core the pears and slice each half into 6-8 wedges. Place in a mixing bowl and toss gently with the lemon juice.

Heat the remaining 1 tbsp oil in a frypan over a high heat. Fry the haloumi slices until they are golden on both sides.

Place watercress or spinach in a large mixing bowl. Add the pears and their juices, the walnuts and their oil (if the walnuts have been baked, add 2 tablespoons olive oil), the fried haloumi and the avocado, if using. Season to taste with salt and pepper then toss gently. Transfer to a serving bowl or individual plates to serve.

Mayonnaise

Mayonnaise is one of the most useful Fridge Fixings. Once you've mastered the basic recipe, have fun with flavourings. For a lovely green sauce, purée a handful of rocket or watercress into the mayonnaise. To add a bit of zing, stir in a dollop of Chilli Jam (see page 128), or to make a luscious aioli, simply add roasted garlic (see below).

Prep time	5 mins
Makes	2½ cups

1 tsp Dijon mustard

1 tsp salt

½ tsp white pepper

3 tbsp lemon juice

3 fresh egg yolks

2 cups grapeseed oil
or half extra virgin olive oil,
half grapeseed oil

Place all the ingredients except the oil in a food processor and blitz to combine. With the motor running, slowly add the oil in a thin stream until the mixture thickens to a creamy sauce. If it gets too thick, thin with a little hot water. Mayonnaise will keep in the fridge for up to 2 weeks.

Roasted Garlic Aioli

Prepare Mayonnaise as above. When thick, blend in the cloves of 1 head of roasted garlic. To roast a head of garlic, separate it into individual cloves, peel them and place them in a small, shallow roasting dish. Pour over enough olive oil to cover the garlic and bake at 150°C for 45 minutes or until soft. I like to make extra roasted garlic and store the rest in its cooking oil in the fridge for later use. It keeps for weeks and the garlic and oil can be used for dressings, sauces and risotto.

Egg and Olive Salad with Aioli

Arrange 4 handfuls (100g) watercress on a serving platter. Top with 4 peeled and halved hard boiled eggs, 2 red peppers that have been roasted, peeled and cut into strips, and 2 tbsp pitted black olives. Drizzle the salad with Roasted Garlic Aioli (see above) and serve. Serves 2 as a light lunch.

When you grow your own food
you feel connected to what you eat
and the rhythms of nature.

Salsa Verde

Most cooks have their own twist on this classic recipe. I prefer not to include mint because I find the flavour too dominant, but I do add the yolk of a boiled egg to give depth to the flavour. The more you blend this sauce the greener it becomes. It's delicious served over grilled vegetables (see below) or with meats such as my Lamb Racks (see page 165).

Prep time	5 mins
Cook time	8 mins
Makes	2 cups

1½ cups (2 handfuls) parsley leaves, de-stemmed

1 handful (about 40) chives, chopped

1 cup extra virgin olive oil

¼ cup capers

3 cloves garlic

4 tbsp lemon juice

2 tsp Dijon mustard

ground black pepper

¼ small red onion, chopped

1 small tin (8-10) anchovies, drained

yolk of one hard boiled egg

Purée all the ingredients in a food processor until smooth. Salsa Verde keeps in a covered jar in the fridge for about a week or it can be frozen.

Grilled Vegetables with Salsa Verde

You can grill pretty much any kind of vegetable. Slice 3 zucchini on an angle into 5mm slices. Core and deseed 2 red or orange peppers and cut into quarters. Scrub or peel 1 large kumara and cut into 5mm slices. Trim 12-15 asparagus spears or green beans and cut 2 red onions into thin wedges. Brush vegetables with extra virgin olive oil and season with salt and ground black pepper. Grill over a medium low heat, turning frequently, until softened and lightly browned. Onions will take about 18-20 minutes, peppers about 10 minutes and asparagus and zucchini about 8 minutes. Pile onto a platter and drizzle with Salsa Verde (see above). Also delicious with Roasted Garlic Aioli (see page 56). Serves 4-6 as a side dish.

Watch Annabel make Salsa Verde at thefreerangecook.com

Harvest Tomato Sauce

This incredibly useful sauce is great tossed through pasta, as a base for soup, added to casseroles and pan sauces, and spread onto bread with cheese for a simple lunch snack. It's brilliant with meatballs (see below) and a tasty base for one of my favourite mussel dishes, Steamed Mussels with Creamy Harvest Sauce (see page 207). I like to make it in bulk when tomatoes are in season and freeze or bottle it.

Prep time	15 mins
Cook time	2 hours
Makes	approx 3 cups

1.5kg tomatoes, cored and cut into wedges

2 red capsicums, deseeded and cut into eighths

1 large onion, cut into thin wedges

4 cloves garlic, peeled

1 tsp chopped rosemary leaves

1 small chilli, seeded and chopped (optional)

¼ cup tomato paste

2 tbsp sugar

2 tbsp extra virgin olive oil

1 tsp salt

ground black pepper

Preheat oven to 160°C. Prepare the tomatoes, capsicums and onion and place them in a large roasting dish lined with baking paper. They need to be in a single layer so they roast and caramelise rather than stew, so use two roasting dishes if necessary.

Add the garlic, rosemary leaves and chilli, if using. In a small bowl mix together the tomato paste, sugar, olive oil, salt and pepper. Spoon this mixture over the vegetables and stir through them to coat evenly.

Bake for about 2 hours or until the vegetables are starting to caramelise and shrivel a little.

Allow the vegetables to cool then purée in a food processor or blender. The sauce will keep in the fridge for up to a week or can be frozen. Alternatively, bring the puréed sauce to a boil and while it is very hot, pour it into sterilised jars. Cover then seal. Sealed jars will keep for months in the pantry.

Spaghetti and Meatballs with Harvest Tomato Sauce

Combine 400g cooked spaghetti and 24 small cooked meatballs in a bowl. Heat together 1½ cups Harvest Tomato Sauce (see above) with ½-¾ cup water and mix through the spaghetti and meatballs. Garnish with chopped Italian parsley and shavings of parmesan cheese. Serves 4-6.

Watch Annabel make Harvest Tomato Sauce at thefreerangecook.com

Tomato Passata

Keep this in the fridge or freezer and stir it into cooked pasta, soups and casseroles.

Prep time	10 mins
Cook time	40 mins
Makes	6 cups

2kg large tomatoes

4 cloves garlic, minced

½ cup extra virgin olive oil

2 tbsp tomato paste

12 basil leaves

1 tsp salt

1 tsp sugar

lots of ground black pepper

It doesn't get much simpler than this! Peel and dice tomatoes. Place all the ingredients in a large pot and simmer over a gentle heat for 40 minutes, stirring occasionally. Cool the sauce, then pass through a mouli or purée in a food processor. Pour into clean jars. The passata will keep in the fridge for over a week or can be frozen for later use.

Fresh Tomato Salsa

This salsa adds a zing to so many dishes, including my Sizzling Beef (see page 150).

Prep time	10 mins
	+ standing
Makes	approx 3 cups

5 tomatoes

2 tbsp coriander or mint

½ medium red onion

1 red chilli

2 cloves garlic

½ tsp salt

2 tbsp lime juice

½ tsp ground black pepper

½ tsp sugar

Core and finely chop the tomatoes. Finely chop the coriander or mint and finely dice the red onion. De-seed and finely mince the chilli. Chop the garlic finely and blend to a paste with the salt using the flat side of a heavy knife.

Mix all the ingredients together in a bowl and leave to stand for at least 30 minutes before serving to allow the flavours to develop. Keep the salsa, covered, in the fridge and use within 3-4 days.

from the garden

Slow Roasted Tomatoes

When you cook tomatoes at a low temperature for a long time you condense and intensify their flavour, giving them a melt-in-the-mouth juiciness. I like to serve them on top of croutons with a salad leaf and Soft Fresh Cheese (see page 222), or as little salads with fresh cheese and pita crisps (see below). I often prepare a double recipe as they can be whizzed up and heated for an instant pasta or steak sauce or soup.

Prep time	5 mins
Cook time	1¼ hours
Serves	6

1kg cherry tomatoes
or 18 small vine tomatoes,
on the vine

¼ cup extra virgin olive oil

2 tbsp balsamic vinegar

½ tsp salt

ground black pepper

2 tsp sugar

Preheat oven to 150°C. Line a baking tray with baking paper and spread the tomatoes out on top. If you are using vine tomatoes, carefully cut the vines into bunches of 3-4 tomatoes, leaving the stems intact.

Drizzle with the oil and vinegar, season with salt and pepper and sprinkle with sugar. Bake for 1¼ hours or until the tomatoes are slightly shrivelled. Leave them on the tray until you are ready to serve them. Serve with the pan juices.

Slow Roasted Tomatoes keep in the fridge for about a week.

Slow Roasted Tomatoes with Fresh Cheese and Pita Breads

Place a handful of salad greens on each of 6-8 plates. Divide 1 recipe Slow Roasted Tomatoes (see above) and 1 recipe Soft Fresh Cheese (see page 222) between the plates. Spoon the juices from the tomatoes over the top and finish with a couple of Crispy Garlic Pita Breads (see below). Serves 6-8.

Crispy Garlic Pita Breads or Croutons

Use the flat side of a heavy knife to crush 2 peeled cloves garlic and ½ tsp salt to a paste. Mix with ⅓ cup olive oil in a small bowl. Split 5 large pita breads or cut a loaf of French bread into rounds about 1cm thick and brush both sides with the oil mixture. Cut pitas into wedges. Spread wedges or croutons on a baking tray. Sprinkle with 1 tsp dried oregano, if desired. Bake in an oven preheated to 150°C until crisp – 25-30 minutes. Store in an airtight container. Makes about 50.

Green Vegetable Toss

This is a zingy accompaniment to Asian chicken, fish or meat dishes. You could add shelled broad beans, green beans or spinach. Asparagus, zucchini, broccoli and beans take longer to cook, so semi-cook them first. If using spinach, add at the last minute.

Prep time	5 mins
Cook time	5-6 mins
Serves	6-8

12-16 spears of asparagus

1 large head broccoli

2-3 zucchini

6 handfuls (200g) snow peas

2 tsp sesame oil

2 tsp grated fresh ginger

3 tbsp water

½ tsp salt

ground black pepper

Trim the asparagus spears and cut each into 2-3 pieces. Cut the broccoli into small florets. Slice the zucchini on an angle into 1cm thick slices. De-string the snow peas.

Heat a pot of lightly salted water. When it boils, add the asparagus, broccoli and zucchini and cook for 2 minutes. Drain, then refresh the vegetables in cold water so they retain their colour and crunch. (The vegetables can be prepared ahead to this point.)

Place the semi-cooked vegetables into a heated pot or frying pan with the snow peas, sesame oil, ginger, water, salt and pepper. Cover and cook for 2-3 minutes or until the snow peas have softened but are still bright green. Serve hot.

Green Beans with Lemon

Par-cooking beans ahead of time ensures you won't have overcooked, grey beans.

Prep time	5 mins
Cook time	6 mins
Serves	6

10-12 handfuls (500-600g) green beans

2 tbsp extra virgin olive oil

finely grated zest of 1 lemon

2-3 tbsp water

salt and ground black pepper

Cut off the stalk ends of the green beans and check for any strings, running a potato peeler down each side if required.

If you like your beans al dente, drop them into a pot of boiling water and cook for 3 minutes. Drain in a colander and cool under cold water. This can be done ahead of time. If you prefer your beans crunchier, skip this step.

When you are ready to serve the dish, heat the oil in a medium saucepan with the lemon zest. Add the beans with the water, salt and pepper. Stir-fry for 2-3 minutes until just tender.

I can sit in the garden and eat snow peas by the bowlful. It's a treat to find a tasty snack that doesn't require opening a packet.

Slow Roasted Tomatoes with
Fresh Cheese and Pita Breads

∿

Crispy Pork Belly
Crunchy New Potatoes with Thyme
Green Beans with Lemon

∿

Honey Vanilla Panna Cotta

Broad Bean Mash with Mint and Parmesan

As well as being a wonderfully healthy side dish, this makes a terrific dip or bruschetta topping and also works well as a pasta sauce thinned with a little of the pasta cooking water. Preparing fresh broad beans is a two-stage process – first remove the beans from the pods, then blanch them and pop the bright green centres out of their thick grey shells. This takes a while but it's quite therapeutic and the beans taste much sweeter for it.

Prep time	15 mins
Makes	approx 2 cups

5 cups de-podded broad beans (about 1kg frozen broad beans or 5kg of fresh broad beans weighed prior to de-podding)

3 cloves garlic, minced

finely grated zest of 2 lemons

24 mint leaves, finely chopped

¼ cup extra virgin olive oil or less, if preferred

½ cup finely grated parmesan, packed firmly

salt and ground black pepper

1-2 tbsp water

If you're using fresh broad beans, bring a large pot of water to the boil and boil the de-podded beans for 2 minutes. Drain and place in a bowl of cool water for easy shucking. If you're using frozen broad beans, put them in a bowl and pour boiling water over the top. Set aside until cool enough to handle.

Slip off the greyish outer skins by grasping each bean by its grooved end and squeezing gently. The bright green inner bean should pop out the other end. Discard the skins. If serving with meat, reserve one cup of beans for a garnish. Otherwise, purée the lot.

Place the beans and all the other ingredients, except the water, in a food processor and pulse to form a very thick purée. The mixture can be prepared ahead of time to this point, and will keep for up to 4 days in the fridge.

When you're ready to eat, heat the beans in a pot, adding the water and stirring frequently until heated through. Adjust the seasonings to taste. Serve hot as a side dish or at room temperature piled onto bruschetta. If serving with meat, scatter the reserved beans around the dish.

Corn and Avocado Salad

When choosing corn cobs look for fresh husks and light brown tassels. If the tassels are very dark brown and shrivelled, you can guarantee the corn will be over-ripe and not nearly as sweet. This salad makes a great side dish for barbecued meat or poultry. You can use frozen or canned corn, but in summer it's really nice to use fresh corn.

Prep time   5 mins
Serves   4

½ cup Basil Oil (see below)
or 2 tbsp basil pesto mixed with
2 tbsp extra virgin olive oil

2 cups cooked corn kernels
(cut from 3 large cobs)

2 tbsp finely chopped red onion

24 cherry tomatoes, halved

1 large just-ripe avocado,
cut into chunks

½ tsp salt

ground black pepper

Toss all the ingredients together and season to taste. The prepared salad can be stored in the fridge for up to 2 hours. If you plan to store it for longer than this, add the avocado at serving time. Return to room temperature before serving.

Fresh Corn on the Cob

Allow 1 corn cob per person. Remove husks from corn and cook in lightly salted boiling water for 3 minutes. Drain and serve hot with butter and salt and ground black pepper.

Basil Oil

Place 2 cups basil leaves in a bowl and cover with boiling water to wilt. Drain at once and refresh the leaves under cold water. Drain again thoroughly, place in a food processor with ½ tsp salt and 1 cup grapeseed or extra virgin olive, or a mix of both, and purée until smooth. You can strain off the solids through a fine sieve, but I don't bother as I like the texture a little rough and rustic. Basil Oil keeps for up to a week in the fridge or can be frozen for later use. Makes 1½ cups.

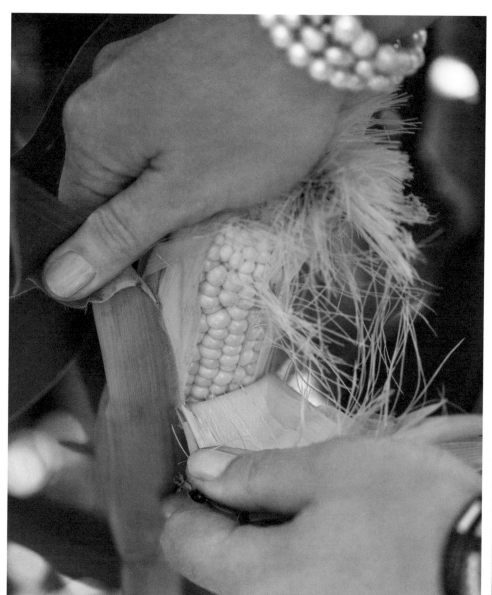

Sometimes you just need to chill out — which is when you need chillies. The hotter the hit, the greater the calming effect chilli has. It also speeds up your metabolism, armours your immunity and gives a zing to your plate.

Chilli Lime Salt

This simple flavoured salt adds zing to fish, chicken, beef or vegetable dishes. It's great sprinkled over sizzling pan fried steaks (see below) or my Barbecued Whole Fish with Chilli Lime Salt (see page 208). For a delicious snack or side dish, simply sprinkle it over baked whole potatoes (see below).

Prep time   5 mins
Makes   ½ cup

1 large fresh red chilli

½ cup flaky sea salt

finely grated zest of 2 limes

Remove seeds from chilli and slice flesh into tiny pieces. Mix with the sea salt and lime zest in a mortar and pestle or food processor and pound or blitz to form a fine crumb. If you want to store the salt for later use, dry it out in the oven at 150°C for 30 minutes.

Baked Potato with Sour Cream and Chilli Lime Salt

Preheat oven to 200°C. Scrub 4 large potatoes and pierce each with a fork several times. Place potatoes in a large bowl and toss with 2 tbsp grapeseed or other neutral oil, ensuring they are coated evenly. Place potatoes in the centre of the oven and bake for 1 hour until crispy and golden. Remove from oven, cut a cross in the top of each potato and pinch the sides a little to open out the cross. Spoon in sour cream and sprinkle with Chilli Lime Salt (see above). Serves 4 as a side dish.

Sizzling Steak with Chilli Lime Salt

Pan fry 4 steaks in a little oil over a high heat for about 2 minutes each side, or to your liking. When steaks are nearly done, sprinkle Chilli Lime Salt (see above) over the top. Serves 4.

Watch Annabel make Chilli Lime Salt at thefreerangecook.com

FRIDGE FIXING

Roasted Pepper Pesto

Pesto is the ultimate Fridge Fixing – so useful to toss through pasta, use as a dip, spread on bruschetta or serve with meat dishes like my Crispy Pork Belly (see page 156). You can make pesto with all sorts of vegetables or herbs, but I especially like this red pepper variation because the paprika gives it a wonderful smoky flavour.

Prep time	20 mins
Cook time	25 mins +
	20 mins cooling
Makes	2 cups

6 red peppers

¼ cup extra virgin olive oil

2 cloves garlic, crushed

1 tsp paprika (plain)

1 tsp smoked paprika

¼ cup almonds, roasted

¼ cup fresh coriander, chopped

salt and ground black pepper

Rinse the peppers and pat dry. Place them on a baking tray and roast at 240°C for about 15-20 minutes until the skin is blistered and blackened. Remove from the oven and cover with a teatowel or put in a plastic bag to sweat. This will make it much easier to remove the skins later. Set aside to cool for about 20 minutes.

While the peppers cool, heat the oil in a small pan and sizzle the garlic and paprika for a few seconds. This helps bring out their flavour. Place this mixture in a food processor or blender.

Remove the skins and seeds from the peppers, saving the juices if you can. Place the flesh and any reserved juices in the food processor or blender with the garlic and paprika mixture. Add the almonds and coriander. Season with salt and pepper and purée until smooth. Pesto will keep in a covered container in the fridge for a week.

Vegetarian Roasted Pepper Pasta with Wilted Spinach

Cook 400-500g dried penne pasta according to the instructions on the packet, then drain. Wash 200g spinach or rocket and cook in a splash of olive oil with a little salt and pepper until wilted – about 2 minutes. Heat 1 cup Roasted Pepper Pesto (see above) and toss through the drained pasta. Divide between 4 serving bowls, top with the wilted greens and garnish with shavings of parmesan. Serves 4.

Beef Kebabs with Roasted Pepper Pesto

Put 8 wooden skewers in water to soak. Cut 600g beef steaks into 2cm cubes. Cut 1 red pepper into 2cm dice and 1 red onion into wedges. Divide into 8 equal portions and thread onto the soaked kebab sticks, alternating beef with red pepper and onion. Season with salt, ground black pepper and 1 tsp cumin. Heat 1 tbsp butter or oil in a heavy based frypan and cook over a high heat for about 2 minutes each side. Serve on steamed rice accompanied by 1 cup Roasted Pepper Pesto (see above). Serves 4.

Watch Annabel make Pepper Pesto at thefreerangecook.com

Fragrant Baked Olives

I often double this recipe so I can serve half and pack half in a jar for another occasion. Served warm, they have a more intense flavour than brined olives and make a great nibble with drinks. I prefer the dense saltiness of Kalamata olives.

Prep time	2-3 mins
Cook time	20 mins
Serves	8-10

40 black Kalamata olives in brine, drained

2 cloves garlic, thinly sliced

2-3 thin strips lemon peel, cut with a vegetable peeler

2-3 thin strips orange peel, cut with a vegetable peeler

1 red chilli, seeds and pith removed, flesh finely chopped

2 whole red chillies

½ tsp fennel seeds

½-¾ cup olive oil

Preheat oven to 180°C. Place the olives in a roasting dish with all the other ingredients and bake for 20 minutes.

Drain, reserving the baking oil, and serve warm.

If packing the olives into a jar, cool and cover with the reserved oil. Top up with extra olive oil if required. They will keep for months and can be reheated to serve.

Soy Roasted Almonds

Home roasted nuts taste much fresher than the store-bought kind. This recipe works well with other nuts too, but watch them closely. The higher the fat content of a nut the more quickly it cooks and the more risk it will burn.

Prep time	5 mins
Cook time	12-15 mins
Makes	2 cups

2 cups (300g) whole almonds

2 tbsp Japanese soy sauce

1 tbsp neutral oil

Preheat oven to 180°C. Place the almonds on a baking tray, pour the soy sauce over the top and mix through evenly. Add the oil and toss to coat.

Roast almonds until they are fragrant and crisp – about 12-15 minutes. Serve immediately or cool before storing in a sealed jar. They will keep for several weeks.

Watch Annabel make Soy Roasted Almonds at thefreerangecook.com

Slow Roasted Red Onions

This is one of those ingenious recipes that you can put on and leave to its own devices, coming back an hour or so later to find it succulent and tender. Red onions are sweeter than white onions, but any kind of onion or shallot loves this treatment.

Prep time	10 mins
Cook time	2-2¼ hours
Serves	6 as a side dish

6 medium red onions, peeled

½ cup water

1 tbsp runny honey

2 tbsp balsamic vinegar

large sprig of thyme, broken up into small sprigs

6 tsp butter

salt and ground black pepper

Preheat oven to 150°C. Cut a thin slice from the top and bottom of each onion and stand them in a lidded casserole dish. Pour the water around them.

Drizzle the onions with honey and vinegar and sprinkle them with thyme sprigs. Top each onion with a teaspoon of butter and season to taste. Cover and bake for 1½ hours.

Remove the lid and continue cooking for a further 30-45 minutes, basting a couple of times during cooking, until the onions are tender but very juicy. This allows the flavour to become really concentrated. Remove from the oven and discard the thyme sprigs before serving the onions with any remaining juices drizzled over the top.

Caramelised Onions

These are useful for all manner of things, so worth making in large quantities. You can use brown or red onions, but red onions are sweeter. Try them also in my Caramelised Onion and Feta Tart (see page 36).

Prep time	5 mins
Cook time	45 mins
Makes	3½ cups

6 red onions

1½ cups water

⅓ cup brown sugar

⅓ cup balsamic vinegar

2 tbsp oil

1 tsp salt

ground black pepper

Peel onions and cut into thin wedges. Place all the ingredients into a large pot and bring to the boil. Reduce heat and simmer gently, stirring now and then, for about 40-45 minutes until the liquid has all but evaporated and the onions are very soft. During the final steps of cooking take care that the onions don't catch and burn. Give them a stir now and then.

Remove from the heat and cool before storing in the fridge in a covered container. Serve at room temperature or reheat in a small pan. Onions will keep, covered, in the fridge for a week.

Caramelised Onion Steak Sauce

In a pan, heat together 1 cup Caramelised Onions (see above) and 1 cup good quality beef stock. Thicken with 2 tsp cornflour mixed with a little water and simmer for 1-2 minutes to cook out the flour. Spoon over grilled steak. Serves 4.

Onion Soup

Heat 1 cup Caramelised Onions (see above) with 2 cups beef stock and simmer for 5 minutes. Meanwhile, sprinkle 4 slices French bread with 2 tbsp grated gruyere cheese and grill until cheese is melted and golden. Divide soup between two bowls and sit croutons on top. Garnish with chopped parsley. Serves 2.

Sausages and Mash with Caramelised Onion Gravy

Cook 4 best quality sausages (such as Italian fennel and pork) in a frypan or oven. In a pot heat 1 cup Caramelised Onions (see above) and ½ cup good quality beef jus or stock. Serve sausages with onion gravy, mashed potatoes and boiled peas. Serves 2.

Watch Annabel make Caramelised Onions at thefreerangecook.com

Potato Gratin with Gruyere and Garlic

Every cook has their own way of making this classic dish and usually it involves lots of careful layering. I have my own 'free range' method, where you simply toss everything together. You can make this recipe ahead of time by baking it for half the time and then finishing it off just before you serve it.

Prep time	10 mins
Cook time	1-1¼ hours
Serves	6

10 (2kg) large potatoes, peeled and sliced 1-1.5cm thick

4 cloves garlic, finely sliced

100g gruyere or cheddar cheese, coarsely grated

1-1½ cups cream

2 tsp salt (more if using flaky salt)

ground black pepper

Preheat oven to 200°C. Grease the base and sides of a shallow 30 x 25cm baking dish. Place the sliced potatoes, garlic, cheese, cream, salt and pepper in the baking dish.

Toss to combine, making sure each potato slice is coated with cream. Spread mixture evenly in the dish. Bake until potatoes are tender and golden – about 1-1¼ hours.

There's a bit of Irish blood in all of us when it comes to potatoes. There are always times when we crave the taste of pure comfort.

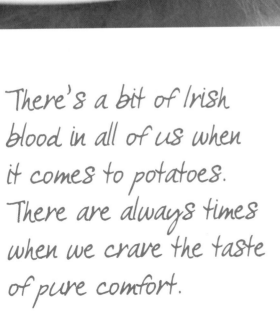

Crunchy Home Made Fries

These moreish oven fries use just a skerrick of oil, making them a healthy adaptation of the traditional deep fried recipe.

Prep time	15 mins
Cook time	1 hour
Serves	6-8

8 medium-large
(130-150g each) potatoes

¼ cup flour

3 tbsp extra virgin olive oil

1 tsp flaky salt

ground black pepper

Preheat oven to 200°C. Line a large, shallow roasting dish with baking paper to allow for easy clean up.

Peel the potatoes and cut into chips or wedges. Transfer to the prepared dish, sprinkle with the flour and toss to evenly combine.

Drizzle the floured potatoes with oil and toss to coat. Spread out into a single layer in the dish and season with salt and pepper. Roast for about 1 hour until golden and crisp.

Crunchy New Potatoes with Thyme

I love the crunchy texture of these potatoes. You only need to break the skin of the potatoes with a fork, not mash them fully. This gives a lovely scrunched surface that crisps up wonderfully and absorbs the herb flavour.

Prep time	5 mins
Cook time	50 mins
Serves	6-8

1.5-2kg baby new potatoes, scrubbed

2 tbsp extra virgin olive oil

2 tsp fresh thyme leaves
or 1 tsp dried thyme

1 tsp flaky sea salt

Preheat oven to 200°C. Boil the potatoes for 10 minutes in lightly salted water. Drain well and transfer to a roasting dish. Use a fork to break the skins and slightly flatten the potatoes.

Drizzle with oil, sprinkle with thyme and flaky salt and roast until crispy and golden – about 40 minutes. Serve hot.

Potato Salad with Capers and Mint

Dress this salad while the potatoes are hot so they better absorb the flavours.

Prep time	10 mins
Cook time	15-20 mins
Serves	6

1-1.2kg baby potatoes

1 tsp Dijon mustard

1 tsp finely grated lemon zest

2 tbsp lemon juice

¼ cup extra virgin olive oil

salt and ground black pepper

1 spring onion

2 tbsp mint

2 tbsp capers

2 tbsp gherkins and 2 tbsp juice

Scrub the potatoes and cut them in half. Simmer in lightly salted water until just tender. Meanwhile, place the mustard, lemon zest and juice, oil and salt and pepper in a jar and shake to combine.

Drain the cooked potatoes and toss with the dressing. Finely chop the spring onion, mint, capers and gherkins and add to the potatoes with the gherkin juice. Toss to mix evenly. Serve warm or cold.

Creamy Coleslaw

Working the thinly sliced cabbage between your fingers makes coleslaw nice and juicy.

Prep time	15 mins
Serves	6-8

½ green cabbage

1 small green capsicum

2 spring onions

3 tbsp parsley

2 tbsp lemon juice

½ cup mayonnaise

3 tsp horseradish

2 tsp rice vinegar

salt and ground black pepper

Core and very finely slice the cabbage. Place in a large mixing bowl and work it between your fingers to soften and moisten. Finely dice the capsicum and finely chop the spring onions and parsley. Add to the cabbage and stir to combine.

To make the dressing, place the lemon juice, mayonnaise, horseradish and rice vinegar in a jar. Add salt and pepper to taste and shake well to combine. Mix through the salad until combined.

Cover the salad and chill until you're ready to serve it. The dressed salad will keep for 24 hours in the fridge, but bring it out of the fridge 15 minutes before serving to allow it to reach room temperature.

Digging in the earth
is such a simple way
to feel grounded.

Braised Red Cabbage

This slightly sweet and sour recipe for red cabbage goes brilliantly with pork dishes like Roast Pork with Fennel, Onions and Apples (see page 159). Never blanch or cook red cabbage in boiling water as you lose the fabulous bright colour.

Prep time	10 mins
Cook time	10-12 mins
Serves	8-10

45-60g (3 tbsp) butter

½ large red cabbage
(800g-1kg), shredded

2 tbsp currants

2 tbsp sugar

1 tsp salt

ground black pepper

2 tbsp red wine vinegar

Melt the butter in a medium to large pot over a medium heat. Add the cabbage, currants, sugar and salt and pepper and stir fry over a medium heat for 10 minutes until the cabbage is wilted and tender.

Mix in the vinegar and adjust the seasonings to taste. Serve immediately or refrigerate and reheat when needed.

Parsnip and Carrot Mash

I love the old-fashioned flavour of this mash, and it's an interesting alternative to plain potato. I also like to use it as a topping on my Cypriot Shepherd's Pie (see page 160).

Prep time	10 mins
Cook time	25-30 mins
Serves	6-8

500g baby carrots or 5-6 large carrots, peeled and diced

4 medium parsnips,
peeled and diced

4 tbsp butter

2 tsp tarragon, chopped

salt and ground black pepper

Boil the carrots and parsnips in lightly salted water until tender – about 25-30 minutes. Drain thoroughly and mash well by hand or blitz in a food processor. Add the butter and tarragon, season with salt and pepper and stir until smooth and well combined. Serve hot.

Vegetable Pakoras

I like to make these tasty snacks using beer as a raising agent as it means I need less soda so I don't get that slightly sour soda taste. They are lovely and light, but you can add a little extra baking soda if you like them even lighter. Make sure you dice the vegetables very finely because they will be in the oil for only a short time to cook through.

Prep time	5 mins + standing
Cook time	3-5 mins per batch
Makes	approx 30

2 cups chickpea or pea flour

2 tsp ground cumin

2 tsp coriander seeds or mustard seeds

1 tsp fennel seeds, roughly ground or chopped

2 tsp curry powder

2 cups beer

½ cup chopped fresh coriander

1½ tsp salt

ground black pepper

¼ tsp baking soda

3 packed cups finely chopped or grated carrot, broccoli, peas, pumpkin, kohlrabi or other vegetables

To fry:
grapeseed, rice bran or other neutral oil

To serve:
Cucumber, Yoghurt and Mint Raita (see page 100) or tamarind sauce or chutney

Combine flour with cumin, coriander or mustard seeds, fennel seeds, curry powder and beer to form a smooth batter. Mix in the chopped fresh coriander, salt and pepper, baking soda, if using, and vegetables. Stand for 5 minutes.

Heat 3-4cm of oil in a deep frypan and fry small spoonfuls of the pakora mixture in batches of 3-5 at a time for about 3 minutes, until golden and cooked through.

Remove the pakoras from the oil with a slotted spoon. Shake off any excess oil and place them on paper towels to drain.

Serve at once, accompanied by Cucumber, Yoghurt and Mint Raita, tamarind sauce or chutney. Pakoras can be prepared ahead and reheated in a 200°C oven for 5 minutes before serving.

Cucumber, Yoghurt and Mint Raita

This refreshing sauce is the perfect accompaniment to serve with my Vegetable Pakoras (see page 99) or any spicy dish.

Prep time   10 mins
Serves   6

1 medium cucumber or
½ telegraph cucumber

1 cup natural yoghurt

small bunch mint (about 40 leaves), chopped

salt and pepper, to taste

To garnish:
a sprig of mint

Peel and de-seed cucumber, then cut into small cubes. Place in a bowl with yoghurt and chopped mint. Stir together then season to taste with salt and pepper. Refrigerate if not using at once. Garnish with mint to serve. Best served the day it is made.

Papaya with Coriander and Lime

Asian food is all about balancing sweet, sour, salty and spicy flavours to create an invigorating harmony on the palate, as this vibrant side dish demonstrates.

Prep time   10 mins
Serves   6

½ papaya or 1 large mango

a small bunch of coriander, chopped

juice of 2 limes

1 red chilli, chopped finely

pinch of sugar

Peel the papaya or mango then either shred with a vegetable peeler or finely slice into ribbons. Place in a bowl with coriander, lime juice chilli and sugar and gently mix together. Refrigerate if not using at once. Best served the day it is made.

Gingered Bok Choy

Like cabbage, bok choy needs brief cooking over a high heat. Dirt often gets trapped at the base of the leaves, so slice each bok choy in half or quarters lengthwise and wash well before cooking.

Prep time	5 mins
Cook time	2-3 mins
Serves	6-8

6-8 whole bok choy

2 tbsp oil

1 tsp grated fresh ginger

2 tbsp water

1 tsp sesame oil (optional)

Halve or quarter bok choy lengthwise and wash well. Place the first measure of oil and the ginger into a large pan or pot. Sauté for a few seconds. Add quartered bok choy, water and sesame oil, if using. Cover and cook until the bok choy is just wilted and translucent – about 2-3 minutes. Serve at once.

You can also drop bok choy into boiling water for 1 minute, cool under cold water and drain before sautéeing in oil with ginger just before serving.

Vegetable Medley

The secret to this dish is to cook the vegetables until they are just tender. Tossing them in butter and lemon just before serving gives them a lovely tang.

Prep time	5 mins
Cook time	5 mins
Serves	8

1 large head broccoli

3 medium zucchini

16-20 baby carrots

¼ cup water

2 tbsp butter

finely grated zest of ½ lemon

salt and ground black pepper

To serve:
1 tsp chopped tarragon
or chervil

Cut broccoli into small florets. Halve zucchini lengthwise then cut on an angle into 1cm slices.

Bring a large pot of salted water to the boil. Add prepared broccoli, zucchini and carrots and boil for 2 minutes. Refresh under cold water and drain well.

When ready to serve, heat water, butter and lemon zest in a large pot or pan. Add vegetables and toss over a high heat for 2-3 minutes until vegetables are just tender. Sprinkle with tarragon or chervil and serve at once.

Creamy Polenta Bake

Sometimes I want a smooth, creamy side dish that's not mashed potatoes. Polenta does the trick. It's just ground cornmeal, so it's handy for people on a wheat-free diet. Because it sets as it cools, it can be made into interesting dishes like Crispy Polenta Wedges (see below). Polenta is quite bland so flavour it with parmesan and herbs.

Prep time	5 mins
Cook time	25-30 mins
Serves	8

9 cups boiling water

3 cups instant polenta

4 tsp salt

½ cup (100g) finely grated parmesan cheese

2 tbsp butter

½ cup cream or milk (optional)

Place the water in a medium saucepan and bring to the boil. Add the polenta in a slow stream, stirring, until the water is fully absorbed. Cover and cook over a low heat for 3 minutes until thickened (take care because it splatters). Stir in the salt, cheese and butter and serve at once as a creamy side dish.

Alternatively, prepare the polenta to this stage then mix in the cream or milk. Spoon it into a shallow baking dish that has been greased with a little butter or oil. Bake for 15 minutes in an oven pre-heated to 180°C, then increase the heat to 220°C for 5-8 minutes to brown the top.

Creamy Basil Polenta

Make the polenta as above and stir in ½ cup basil pesto. Serve at once.

Crispy Polenta Wedges

Grease a shallow 20cm square baking tray or tin. Pour in 1 quantity of cooked Creamy Polenta (see above), ensuring it is evenly spread. Leave to cool for about 40 minutes. Refrigerate for another 30-40 minutes until firm, or overnight. When you are ready to eat, cut the polenta into 5cm slices or wedges or shapes of your choice. Roll in polenta grains to coat. Heat a little oil in a frypan and cook in batches until lightly browned.

Couscous with Roasted Vegetables

The hallmark of a good cook is resourcefulness. It's easy to cook with fancy ingredients, but to make something really delicious out of basic ingredients takes thought and imagination. This makes a great side dish, or even a vegetarian main.

Prep time	10 mins
	+ 10 mins
	standing
Cook time	45 mins
Serves	6

2 red onions, peeled

3 medium beetroots, peeled, or 10-12 baby beetroots, scrubbed

200g pumpkin, skin and seeds removed

6 small or 3 medium carrots, peeled

2 kumara or other sweet potato, peeled (optional)

3 tbsp extra virgin olive oil

2 tbsp maple syrup or golden syrup or honey

salt and ground black pepper

2 cups couscous

finely grated zest of 1 lemon

1 tsp salt

2 cups boiling water

½ packed cup mint leaves (about 50 leaves), chopped or torn

¼ cup lemon juice

½ cup shelled unsalted pistachio nuts, chopped

Preheat oven to 180°C. Halve the onions lengthwise and cut into 2cm wedges. Cut the medium beetroot into 2cm chunks or the baby beets into quarters. Cut the pumpkin, carrots and kumara or sweet potato, if using, into 2cm chunks.

Place the prepared vegetables in a very large roasting dish or two and spread out to a single layer. Drizzle with oil and maple syrup or golden syrup or honey and season with salt and pepper to taste. Roast for about 45 minutes or until the vegetables are tender and starting to caramelise.

In a large bowl, mix the couscous, lemon zest, salt and boiling water. Allow to stand for about 10 minutes, then fluff up with a fork.

Add the roasted vegetables, mint and lemon juice to the couscous and toss gently to combine. Transfer to a serving bowl and garnish with the chopped pistachios.

Couscous with Grapes and Cranberries

Almonds, grapes and cranberries are tossed through couscous to create perfect picnic fare.

Prep time   10 mins
+ standing
Serves   6 as a side dish

1½ cups boiling water

pinch of saffron threads

1½ cups couscous

finely grated zest of 1 lemon

finely grated zest of ½ orange

1 tsp salt

½ cup slivered almonds, toasted

2 cups chopped green grapes

½ cup chopped dried cranberries

¼ cup chopped mint

3 tbsp Dijon Vinaigrette Dressing (see page 49)

Put the boiling water and saffron in a cup and leave to stand for at least 5 minutes.

In a large bowl mix together the couscous, lemon zest, orange zest, salt and saffron water. Allow to stand for about 10 minutes, then fluff up with a fork.

Add the almonds, grapes, cranberries, mint and dressing and toss to combine.

Couscous and Apricot Stuffing

In a bowl mix together 1 cup couscous, finely grated zest of 1 lemon, 1 tsp salt and 1 cup boiling water. Allow to stand for about 10 minutes, then fluff up with a fork. Add 2 tsp fresh thyme leaves (or 1 tsp dried thyme), ½ cup chopped parsley, ¼ cup pinenuts and 8-10 finely chopped dried apricot halves. Toss to combine with 2 tbsp melted butter. Makes 3 cups stuffing – enough for 4 poussins or 1 large chicken.

Harissa

There are as many recipes for this spice paste as there are cooks in North Africa, but this is my favourite variation. The rosewater adds a delicate floral accent. It's delicious stirred into couscous, stews and soups, or rubbed onto meat before grilling or barbecuing.

Prep time	15 mins
Cook time	2-3 mins
Makes	1 cup

2 tsp coriander seeds

1 tsp cumin seeds

4 cloves garlic

1-2 hot chillies

1 tsp flaky salt

¼ cup oil

1 tsp cayenne pepper

1 cup tomato purée

2 tsp rosewater or a pinch of sugar

Toast the coriander and cumin seeds in a dry frypan until they just start to pop – watching closely so you don't burn them. Grind the toasted seeds with a mortar and pestle.

Chop the garlic and chillies and crush them into a paste with the salt.

Return crushed seeds to the frypan, add oil, chilli and garlic paste and cayenne pepper. Sizzle for a few seconds then add tomato purée. Simmer over a high heat for a couple of minutes until the mixture thickens. Remove from heat and mix in rosewater or sugar.

Store harissa in the fridge covered with a film of oil – it will keep for a couple of weeks.

Watch Annabel make this recipe at thefreerangecook.com

South East Asian Curry Base

You can buy very acceptable curry bases these days, but it's certainly more economical to make your own. My favourite is this South East Asian version, which is more aromatic than a spicy Indian curry mix. Don't be daunted by the list of ingredients – once you've compiled them your work is done – the food processor does the rest for you.

Prep time	10 mins
Makes	5 cups

4 large onions

1 whole hand of ginger

1 whole head garlic

4 green chillies, or more to taste

2 Kaffir lime leaves, finely chopped, or extra zest of 2 limes

2 cups roughly chopped coriander, roots included if available

grated zest of 3 limes

1 cup grapeseed, rice bran or other neutral oil

2 tsp blachan/dried shrimp paste

1 tsp dried chilli flakes

3 tsp ground cumin

1 tsp coriander seed

2 tsp turmeric

1 tbsp fish sauce

Peel and chop onions and ginger. Break garlic into cloves and peel.

Discard seeds from green chillies and finely chop the chillies. Remove central rib from kaffir lime leaves, destem and finely chop.

Place all the ingredients into a food processor and blend to a paste.

This curry base can be made several days ahead of time and refrigerated. It can also be frozen.

Vegetarian Curry

Gently fry 2 cups South East Asian Curry Base (see above) in a large pot for 5-10 minutes then stir in 2 cups coconut milk. Add 250g peeled and diced pumpkin, 2 red onions cut into wedges, 250g cubed potato, kumara or sweet potato, 1 sliced red pepper and 1 cubed eggplant and simmer until tender – 20-30 minutes. Add 1 cup peas or beans and cook 5 minutes. Serve on rice. Serves 4 as part of a shared meal.

Silverbeet, Feta and Pinenut Roll

Silverbeet is the easiest thing to grow and superbly nutritious. I love it combined with pinenuts and cheeses in this delicious pie. Don't freak out when you see how much silverbeet you need to start with – it will cook down to much less. I like to use a combination of cheeses to give a nice balance of tastes – bite from the parmesan, bulk from the ricotta and creaminess from the feta.

Prep time	15 mins
Cook time	40 mins
Serves	6

250g silverbeet or spinach

2 tbsp butter

1 large onion, finely chopped

1 cup ricotta

¾ cup feta, crumbled

½ cup grated parmesan

¼ cup chopped coriander

½ tsp ground nutmeg

finely grated zest of ½ lemon

⅓ cup pinenuts, toasted

½ tsp salt

ground black pepper

1 egg, lightly beaten

8 sheets filo pastry

melted butter or oil spray

Preheat oven to 180°C. Trim half of the white stalks from the silverbeet and discard them. Wash, dry and chop the leaves and the rest of the stalks.

Heat the butter in a medium pot and cook the onion over a low heat until it is soft but not browned – about 5 minutes. Add the silverbeet and cook until the water from the leaves evaporates, leaving the pan dry. Removing the moisture from the silverbeet in this way helps to stop the pie going soggy.

Remove the pot from the heat and mix in the ricotta, feta, parmesan, coriander, nutmeg, lemon zest and pinenuts. Season to taste with salt and pepper. Stir in the egg.

Place a sheet of filo pastry on the bench. Brush it with melted butter or spray it liberally with oil. Place a second sheet on top and brush it with butter or spray it with oil. Repeat to form a stack of 8 pastry sheets. The filo dries out quickly so you will need to work fast. Cover the unused filo with a damp teatowel while you work.

Form the silverbeet mixture into a sausage shape along the longest edge of the pastry, leaving a 3cm border at the sides.

Turn in the sides of the pastry like an envelope and roll it up gently and loosely to fully enclose the filling, forming a log shape. If you roll it too tight it will split. Transfer the log to a baking tray, brush the top with butter and bake until it is golden and crisp – about 40 minutes.

Goat Cheese and Spinach Soufflés

These twice baked soufflés take the hassle out of soufflé making. Double baking means you can serve up light-as-air soufflés without having to wait half an hour for them to cook at the last minute.

Prep time	15 mins
Cook time	15-20 mins for first baking + 10-12 mins for second stage
Serves	6-8

50g butter, plus extra to butter ramekins or cups

½ cup flour

2 cups milk

pinch freshly ground nutmeg

salt and ground pepper

5 egg yolks

¾ cup coarsely grated goat feta

¼ cup finely grated parmesan

½ cup cooked spinach, squeezed to remove excess water then very finely chopped

5 egg whites

To finish:
6-8 tbsp cream

First preheat the oven to 175°C, then generously butter 6-8 one cup ramekins and put in the fridge to chill.

Melt the butter in a medium saucepan. Stir in the flour and cook, stirring, for about 2 minutes without browning. Whisk in the milk, nutmeg, salt and pepper and bring the sauce to a boil, stirring constantly, until it thickens.

Simmer, stirring, over a low heat, for 2 minutes. The mixture will be very thick. Taste for seasoning – it should taste highly seasoned. Remove the pot from the heat and beat in the egg yolks one at a time. Fold in the feta, parmesan and spinach.

Place the egg whites in a clean, dry bowl and beat until they form soft peaks. Add one quarter of the egg whites to the sauce and stir until well mixed. Fold remaining egg whites gently through.

Set the buttered ramekins in a deep roasting dish. Fill ramekins, then run your thumb around the inside edges to help the soufflés puff evenly. Pour boiling water into the roasting dish until it comes about half way up the sides of the soufflé dishes. This will help the soufflés to cook evenly.

Bake until the soufflés are puffed, browned and just set in the centre – about 15-20 minutes. (They can be cooked through at this point. Simply leave them in the oven to cook for another 5-10 minutes.)

If not serving at once, take the soufflés out of the water bath and leave to cool. They will shrink back into the ramekins. Cover and place in the fridge for up to 24 hours. To reheat, either leave them in their dishes or unmould into an ovenproof dish. Heat oven to 220°C. Drizzle cream over soufflés and bake until browned and slightly puffed – about 10-12 minutes. Serve immediately.

Roasted Beet and Rocket Salad

∽

Beef Steak and Double Mushroom Sauce
Potato Gratin with Gruyere and Garlic
Green Beans with Lemon

∽

Sticky Date Pudding
with Wicked Toffee Sauce

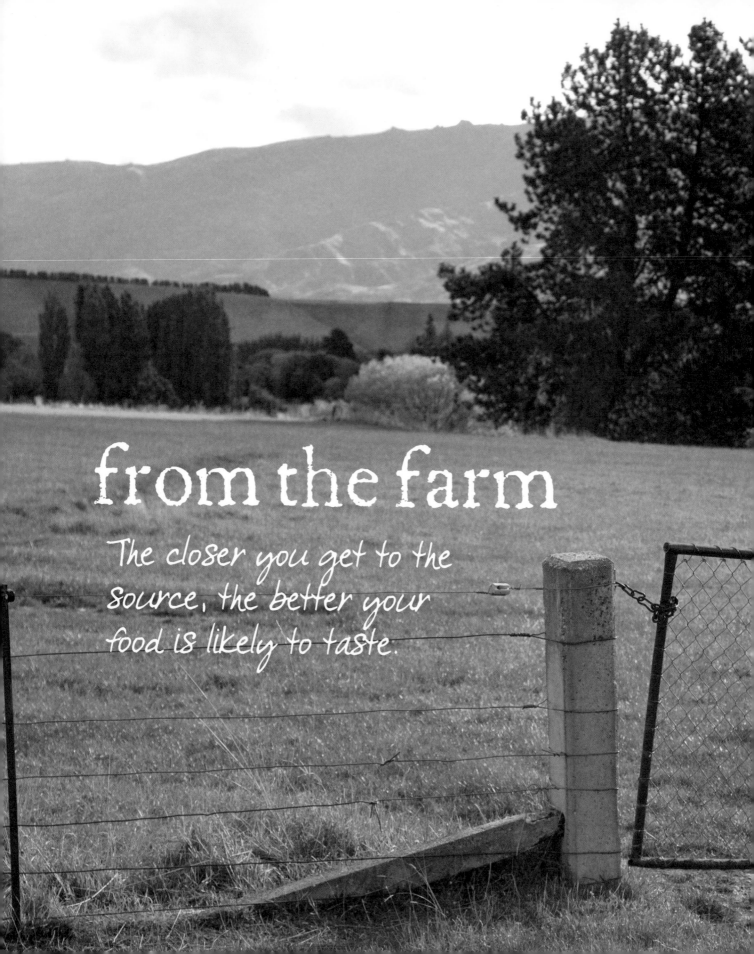

from the farm

The closer you get to the source, the better your food is likely to taste.

When I met the man who was to become my husband, he was a shepherd in the back blocks of the East Coast, north of Gisborne. On the occasional trip to town he would bring the 13 working dogs on his team, stopping at the local burger bar for a standing order of 14 egg burgers – Beth, his favourite, always got two.

My husband Ted grew up riding his pony to school each day. For after-school fun he and his sisters would raid the pantry for jelly crystals, sneak the candlewick bedspreads off the beds and ride off into the scrub, swooping down on the small calves in the home paddock in whooping Indian raids.

With a 'picnic' of nothing more than a can of herrings in tomato sauce, a loaf of bread, tea leaves and sugar, Ted and his sisters would ride out to the back of the farm, moving stock and fixing fences from dawn till dusk, following the glowing tip of their father Rob's rollie cigarette back through the scrub on the dark ride home.

Trips to town to buy groceries and farm supplies were made every two or three weeks – tea, sugar, flour, salt, rice, canned herrings, condensed milk and jelly crystals pretty well summed up the family grocery list – everything else they grew or made themselves. In this spirit of resourcefulness, the family thrived and prospered, using their savings to buy more farms – an Irish heritage resonating through the generations. Ted's grandmother would send the wool from the family's sheep off to a mill in England to get woven into bolts of cloth, and the entire family would end up kitted out in the same fabric for a couple of years at a time.

It requires a certain degree of fatalism to be a farmer. So much is unpredictable – droughts, floods, frosts and market prices, all are out of your control.

The best you can do is ensure your stock are in the best possible condition – animals that roam free and healthy with fresh grass to graze always make for good eating.

There is a duty of care and respect in the noble profession of farming. Everything we eat starts as a seed or spore, often taking months or even years to reach maturity. In the hands of our farmers rests not just the quality of our food, but the ongoing health of our land and water.

Ted's father Rob was a stickler for quality and the best meat was always saved for the family, perfectly aged and beautifully butchered.

Today meat from our farm still hangs dry in the chiller to age for at least a week before it gets cut down for the table. Steak is never cut into steaks until it is ready to be cooked – it ages better in the piece. Kept dry and cold, a carcass will keep for several weeks but get it wet or put plastic anywhere near it and it goes off fast. A good butcher knows all this and more, and cultivating a relationship with your butcher is key to getting quality and value when buying meat.

When it comes to cooking, choose the right cut for the job. The muscles that work hardest, like the shanks, shins, cheeks and tails, are by nature tough and sinewy, but given long, slow cooking they render the most flavour, with fabulous succulence and tenderness. Their connective tissue breaks down completely, giving the meat a melt-in-the-mouth quality.

The two eye fillets in each animal are the tenderest, most expensive cuts, but actually the least flavoursome. The cheaper sirloin is, to my mind, the tastiest of the tender cuts and my preference for quick cooking every time.

Just one simple
ingredient,
be it a spice,
a fruit or a
condiment,
can bring the
flavour of
a new culture
into your
everyday life.

Pork Rillettes with Prune Topping

I enjoy experimenting to see whether I can come up with leaner and less time consuming versions of classic dishes – the challenge here was to lose some of the fat but not the depth of flavour. This recipe makes five dishes, each big enough to serve six as an appetiser.

Prep time	10 mins
Cook time	3 hours
Makes	five 1-cup dishes

800g skinless pork slices
or skinless pork belly
cut into finger-wide strips

3 cloves garlic

1 tsp salt

2 bay leaves

1 small bunch thyme
or tarragon

2 whole star anise

½ tsp ground black pepper

½ cup white wine

¼ cup brandy

Prune topping:
250g pitted prunes

1 cup red wine

2 tbsp sugar

¼ tsp ground cloves

Preheat oven to 150°C. Arrange pork in a single layer in a shallow baking dish. Crush garlic to a paste with the salt using the flat side of a heavy knife on a chopping board and rub the paste over the meat. Scatter with the herbs and star anise and season with pepper. Pour the wine and brandy over the pork.

Cut a piece of baking paper to cover the pork snugly, place it over the meat then cover the entire dish with a lid or a tight seal of foil. Bake for 3 hours.

While the pork cooks, prepare the prune topping. Place the prunes in a small pot with the red wine, sugar and ground cloves. Cook for 12 minutes, then mash or purée until smooth, adding 2-3 tbsp of water as needed to achieve a thick, jam-like consistency.

Remove the cooked pork from the oven and discard the herbs and star anise. Cool the meat then roughly cut it up and place it in a food processor with 3-4 tbsp of the cooking liquid. Pulse to form a coarse, rough purée (don't blend to a smooth paste).

Divide pork rillettes into five 1-cup serving dishes, each about ¾ full. Spread the prune topping in a 1cm layer over the top. Cover and chill in the fridge for at least 24 hours or up to 10 days. It can also be frozen. Serve with Melba Toasts (see below).

Melba Toasts

Preheat oven to 150°C. Cut the crusts from 1 loaf thinly sliced bread (wholemeal works well) and flatten each slice with a rolling pin. Cut each slice in half diagonally. Spread the bread triangles on a baking tray and bake until very crisp and dry – about 20-25 minutes. Allow to cool then store in an airtight container. If they get a little stale refresh for 5 minutes in an oven preheated to 150°C. Makes 4 dozen.

Chilli Jam

I like to make this in autumn when the chillies are ripe in my garden. There are lots of varieties of chillies, all with different levels of heat. The rule of thumb is usually the smaller, the hotter. If you prefer a milder sauce, use 2-3 chillies and a large red pepper.

Prep time	10 mins
Cook time	10 mins
Makes	1 jar (2 cups)

1 head garlic, cloves peeled

6-8 long red chillies, roughly chopped

3 thumb-sized pieces (200g) fresh ginger, peeled and roughly chopped

2 double kaffir lime leaves, deveined (optional)

2½ cups caster sugar

½ cup water

finely grated zest of 4 limes

½ cup rice vinegar

3 tbsp fish sauce

1 tsp soy sauce

Sterilise a 2-cup screw top jar and its metal lid.

Purée the garlic, chillies, ginger and kaffir lime leaves, if using, to a coarse paste. Place in a saucepan with the sugar, water, lime zest, rice vinegar, fish sauce and soy sauce.

Stir over a medium heat until the sugar dissolves, then boil for about 10 minutes until reduced by a third. It will bubble up like jam.

Spoon the hot chilli jam into the warm sterilised jar until it is filled to within 3mm of the top. Seal with the screw lid. Once opened, store Chilli Jam in the fridge. It will keep for months.

Crudites with Chilli Jam Dipping Sauce

Spoon 3 tbsp Chilli Jam (see above) into a small dish. Slice 2 carrots, 3 sticks of celery and 1 Lebanese cucumber or ⅓ telegraph cucumber into batons. Place the Chilli Jam in the centre of a large platter and pile the vegetable batons around the outside to serve. Serves 4 as a snack.

Roasted Chicken Wings or Drumsticks

Preheat oven to 180°C. Place 16 chicken wings, drumsticks or nibbles in an ovenproof dish. Add about 4 tbsp Chilli Jam (see above) and stir to coat chicken. Spread out in a single layer and bake for 30-40 minutes or until golden and cooked. Sprinkle with chopped fresh coriander and serve. Serves 4-6.

Watch Annabel make Chilli Jam at thefreerangecook.com

Fragrant Baked Olives
Soy Roasted Almonds
Sesame and Oregano Lavosh

∽

Roast Pork with
Fennel, Onions and Apples
Creamy Polenta Bake
Braised Red Cabbage

∽

Verjuice Nectarine Jelly

Chicken, Eggplant and Green Bean Korma

If you have ever been nervous about cooking a South East Asian meal then this is the one to try. It is a wonderfully fragrant one pot meal that your friends and family are sure to love. Serve it with rice.

Prep time   20 mins
Cook time   40 mins
Serves   4-5

2 cups South East Asian
Curry Base (see page 112)

3 cups chicken stock

1 cup coconut cream

1 heaped tsp brown sugar
or grated palm sugar

salt and ground black pepper

3-4 Japanese eggplants,
sliced into 2cm pieces
or 400g regular eggplant,
sliced into 2-3cm pieces

1kg boneless, skinless chicken
thighs, cut in half

2 tomatoes, chopped

400g green beans,
trimmed and cut into thirds

½ cup cashew nuts,
roasted and ground

To serve:
steamed rice

poppadoms

Place the South East Asian Curry Base in a large pot and fry it slowly for 15 minutes, stirring frequently until very soft but not browned.

Add the stock, coconut cream and sugar, and salt and pepper to taste. Stir to incorporate and bring to the boil.

Add the eggplant and simmer for 10 minutes. Add the chicken thighs and simmer for another 10 minutes. Add tomatoes, beans and half the ground cashew nuts and cook for a further 5-6 minutes until the beans are just tender.

Spoon into a serving dish and sprinkle with the remaining cashew nuts to serve. Serve with steamed rice and poppadoms.

Pan-fried Chicken with Verjuice Glaze

This simple variation on pan-fried chicken breasts uses Verjuice (see page 287) and green peppercorns to create a deliciously tangy sauce. Serve with mashed potato and lightly cooked greens for a quick and easy meal. Deglazing is a method by which liquid is used to loosen the flavoursome cooked chicken brownings from the inside of the pan to make a sauce.

Prep time	5 mins
Cook time	20-25 mins
Serves	2

2 single boneless chicken breasts

salt and ground black pepper

2 tbsp butter

1 tbsp green peppercorns

½ cup Verjuice
(see page 287)
or white wine

¼ cup cream (optional)

Place the chicken breasts between two pieces of waxed paper and lightly flatten with a rolling pin. Season the chicken with salt and pepper to taste.

Heat the butter in a frypan and brown the chicken for about 10 minutes on each side.

Add the peppercorns and Verjuice or wine to the pan and stir to deglaze the pan. Simmer for 2-3 minutes to reduce the sauce to a shiny glaze. Add the cream, if using, and boil again for a minute to lightly thicken. Serve glaze hot, poured over the chicken.

Baked Lemon Grass and Chilli Chicken

This is my go-to meal when time is tight. It takes only a few minutes to throw together and cooks in the oven while you prepare some rice and vegetables and set the table. The sauce also works well with a butterflied whole chicken (cook for 50-60 minutes) or fillets of fresh fish (cook for 8-10 minutes).

Prep time	10 mins
Cook time	30-35 mins
Serves	6

6-8 single boneless chicken breasts, skin on

3 tsp finely grated lemon grass

½ cup sweet chilli sauce

¼ cup water

2 tbsp fish sauce

2 kaffir lime leaves, finely chopped
or finely grated zest of 2 limes

2 tbsp lime juice

2 cloves garlic, crushed

To serve:
steamed jasmine rice

1 recipe Green Vegetable Toss
(see page 68)

Preheat oven to 200°C. Place chicken breasts skin side up in a shallow baking dish. Combine all other ingredients in a small bowl and pour over the chicken.

Bake until chicken is cooked through and golden – about 30-35 minutes. To check whether the chicken is done, insert a clean skewer into the thickest part of one chicken breast. If the juices run clear, it is cooked. If they are pink, return the dish to the oven and cook a little longer before testing again.

Serve with jasmine rice and Green Vegetable Toss.

Variation

If you have a jar of my super Chilli Jam (see page 128) in the fridge you can make an even quicker chilli sauce for chicken. Simply mix ½ cup Chilli Jam with ¼ cup water and 2 tbsp lime juice. Pour over the chicken and cook as described above.

People love it
when you cook
for them, no
matter how
simple the fare.
Food always
tastes good
cooked over
a fire and
eaten outside.

Spicy Rub

This rub is marvellous on any cuts of meat or chicken, including my Barbecued Lamb (see page 148). It's also great stir-fried with chickpeas or stirred into yoghurt as a sauce, dressing or dip (see below).

Prep time	5 mins
Cook time	1 min
Makes	2 cups

6 cloves garlic, crushed

finely grated zest of 2 lemons

¾ cup lemon juice

2 fresh chillies,
very finely chopped

3 tbsp finely grated ginger

½ cup extra virgin olive oil

2 tbsp ground cumin

2 tsp ground turmeric

2 tsp paprika

2 cinnamon quills,
roughly broken

2 tsp sugar

2 tsp salt

½ tsp black pepper

Place the garlic, lemon zest and juice, chillies and ginger in a small bowl and mix to combine.

Heat the oil in a frypan and fry the cumin, turmeric, paprika and cinnamon quills over a medium heat for about 30 seconds to toast and release aromas. Don't let them burn.

Add the garlic and ginger mixture and cook for another 30-40 seconds over a low heat, just to sizzle. Remove from the heat and mix in the sugar and salt and pepper. Allow to cool.

This recipe makes enough for several meals. If not using immediately, store in a covered container in the fridge. It will keep for weeks.

Spicy Yoghurt Dip

In a small bowl mix together 1 tbsp Spicy Rub (see above), 1 cup Greek yoghurt and 1 tbsp lemon juice. Keeps in the fridge for about a week. Makes 1 cup.

Spicy Chickpea and Pepper Stirfry

Heat 2 tbsp Spicy Rub (see above) in a frypan. Add 2 x 300g cans chickpeas and 2 thinly sliced red peppers and cook until coated in spice mixture and warmed through. Add 200g baby spinach leaves and cook until wilted. Garnish with a handful of coriander leaves before serving. Serves 4 as a side dish.

Recipes that can take you in lots of different directions are always useful. A marinade transforms into a dip, a sauce or a dressing.

Spicy Chicken Skewers

There's something about food on skewers that's irresistible to most people – especially children. These spicy skewers are marinated in half a recipe of my incredibly versatile Chermoula Marinade (see page 144). Use the other half to make Chermoula Dipping Sauce to serve on the side and toss through a cucumber salad (see below).

Prep time	10 mins + up to 24 hours marinating
Cook time	10-12 mins
Serves	6-8

10 (1.2kg) boneless chicken thighs, cut into thirds or quarters

½ recipe Chermoula Marinade (see page 144)

To serve:
1 recipe Creamy Moroccan Cucumber Salad (see below)

½ recipe Chermoula Dipping Sauce (see page 144)

Place the chicken pieces in a bowl and stir through the Chermoula Marinade. Marinate the chicken in the fridge for at least one hour or up to 24 hours.

Soak 20 wooden chopsticks in water for at least half an hour. When you are ready to cook the chicken lift it out of the marinade and slide 2-3 pieces onto each skewer. Shake off and discard any leftover marinade (because it contains the juices of raw chicken this cannot be reused).

Lightly oil a frypan or barbecue hotplate and cook the chicken over a medium heat for about 5-6 minutes on each side, or until fully cooked and golden.

Transfer the cooked skewers to a serving plate and serve immediately, accompanied by the Creamy Moroccan Cucumber Salad and a bowl of Chermoula Dipping Sauce.

Creamy Moroccan Cucumber Salad

In a bowl combine 1 diced telegraph cucumber with 400g halved cherry tomatoes and ½ recipe (about 1 cup) Chermoula Dipping Sauce (see page 144). Serves 6 as a side dish.

Chermoula Marinade

This is a delicious marinade for any kind of meat, poultry or seafood. Try it on my Spicy Chicken Skewers (see page 142). Add yoghurt or sour cream to make Chermoula Dipping Sauce (see below), which is one of those very yummy, useful things to slather or dip. I use it to dress Creamy Moroccan Cucumber Salad (see page 142) and Spicy Casbah Prawns (see page 176). The Preserved Lemons (see page 304) give a lovely tang to the marinade and the dipping sauce.

Prep time	10 mins
Makes	approx 2 cups

2 cloves garlic, crushed

2 tbsp finely chopped fresh ginger

1 tsp ground ginger

¼ tsp cayenne pepper

2 tsp ground cumin

2 tsp brown sugar

1 tsp salt

juice and finely grated zest of 2 lemons

1 cup unsweetened runny natural yoghurt

½ cup coriander leaves, tightly packed

2 tbsp Preserved Lemons (see page 304), finely chopped (optional)

Place all ingredients except the Preserved Lemons in a food processor or blender and whiz until smooth. Stir in the chopped Preserved Lemons, if using (the texture is nicer if this isn't blended). Chermoula Marinade will keep in a covered container in the fridge for 5-6 days.

Chermoula Dipping Sauce

In a bowl mix 1 cup sour cream or Greek yoghurt into ½ recipe Chermoula Marinade (see above). Refrigerate until ready to serve. Makes about 2 cups.

Fresh ingredients and
good company are
a proven recipe for fun.
It's not about fancy
culinary gymnastics.

Cooking at home connects us
with friends and family, nature
and our own creativity.

Barbecued Lamb with Spicy Rub

Ask your butcher to bone and butterfly a leg of lamb for this dish. Butterflying the meat flattens it out and ensures quick and even cooking. The exotic, smoky flavours of this lamb are delicious served with my Spicy Yoghurt Dip (see page 140) and Couscous with Roasted Vegetables (see page 106).

Prep time	5 mins
	+ marinating
Cook time	40-50 mins
	+ resting
Serves	6-8

1 whole leg of lamb, boned and butterflied open

about ¾ cup Spicy Rub (see page 140)

salt and ground black pepper

To garnish:
½ cup chopped fresh mint or coriander

Trim the meat of excess fat and place it in a clean plastic bag with the Spicy Rub. Seal the bag and refrigerate for at least 2 hours or up to 48 hours, turning occasionally.

Preheat the barbecue grill over a medium-high heat. Remove the meat from the bag and season it with salt and pepper. Place on the hot grill and cook until lightly browned – about 5 minutes each side.

Weight the meat with a large, clean stone or a brick wrapped in foil or place a tray on top of the meat and weigh it down with a couple of heavy stones or a brick. Lower the heat and cook for a further 15-20 minutes on each side or until it is done to your liking.

Remove the lamb from the heat, cover and rest for 10 minutes before carving in thin slices across the grain. Sprinkle with coriander or mint to serve.

Sizzling Beef & Salsa

Creating a relaxed atmosphere is the key to entertaining. If you're stressed out about a complicated recipe, there's no way you or your friends are going to have a good time. This dish is incredibly simple but it looks like a million bucks, and best of all you do most of the work in advance. It makes a great meal with Crusty Flat Bread (see page 18), Crunchy Home Made Fries (see page 91) and Creamy Coleslaw (see page 92). Chicken or pork can be used instead of beef.

Prep time	10 mins
	+ marinating
Cook time	3 mins
	+ 5 mins resting
Serves	6-8

1.3-1.5kg sirloin or rump steak

2 tsp cumin seeds

1 tsp chilli powder

1 tsp ground cumin

1 tsp paprika

½ tsp ground black pepper

½ tsp sugar

½ tsp fresh rosemary, finely chopped

3 cloves garlic, peeled

1 tsp salt

2 tbsp extra virgin olive oil

1 recipe Fresh Tomato Salsa (see page 64)

To garnish:
fresh coriander, chopped

Cut the sirloin or rump into 6-8 steaks, each about 3cm thick.

Toast the cumin seeds in a dry frypan until they pop, being careful not to burn them. Place them in a small bowl with the chilli powder, ground cumin, paprika, pepper, sugar and rosemary. Crush the garlic and salt into a fine paste using the flat side of a heavy knife. Mix the garlic paste into the spices.

Massage the spice mixture all over the steak, cover and allow to stand for at least 30 minutes or for up to 12 hours in the fridge.

When you are ready to eat, heat the oil in a heavy-based frypan and fry the steaks over a high heat for 1½ minutes on each side. They should be rare inside. Lift them out of the pan and place them on a board to rest for 5 minutes.

Remove any visible fat then angle cut each steak into about 5-6 slices. Place in a bowl with the cooking juices and mix in half the Fresh Tomato Salsa.

Heat a cast iron pan over the highest heat. When the pan is super hot, add meat and salsa, garnish with coriander and take, sizzling, to the table at once. Serve the rest of the salsa in a separate dish.

Beef Steak and Double Mushroom Sauce

Steak and mushrooms are a perfect combination and this recipe is a way of taking the last-minute hassle out of cooking steak. You can brown the steaks up to a day ahead and keep them in the fridge. Bring them back to room temperature for 20 minutes before finishing in the oven. You can also make the sauce in advance – it reheats well. Cut steak from a well aged piece for maximum tenderness and flavour.

Prep time	10 mins
	+ soaking
Cook time	20 mins
	+ 5 mins resting
Serves	6

6 aged beef steaks, such as sirlion, about 4cm thick

salt and ground black pepper

6 tsp butter

12 sliced dried mushrooms, such as porcini or shiitake

½ cup port, red wine or water

500g fresh field or portabello mushrooms, sliced

2 fat cloves garlic, thinly sliced

2 cups good quality beef stock

1 tbsp cornflour
mixed with 2 tbsp water

To garnish:
fresh coriander

To serve:
Potato Gratin with Gruyere and Garlic (see page 88)

Green Beans with Lemon (see page 68)

Season steaks with salt and pepper and tie a piece of string firmly around the circumference of each one so they hold their shape while cooking. Spread a teaspoon of butter on one side of each steak. Heat a frypan over a high heat and when it is very hot cook each steak, butter side down, for 1 minute. Turn and cook the other side for a minute more. You want to just brown them.

Remove steaks from pan and transfer to an oven tray lined with baking paper. They can be prepared to this point up to a day ahead.

Place the dried mushrooms in a bowl, pour in the port, red wine or water and leave to soak for at least 15 minutes.

When you are ready to eat, preheat oven to 200°C and remove the steaks from the fridge to bring them back to room temperature. Add the sliced fresh mushrooms to the frypan in which the steaks were cooked. Sauté, stirring often, until they are lightly browned and the pan is dry – about 5-10 minutes.

Add garlic to the pan and cook for a few seconds. Add soaked dried mushrooms plus their soaking liquid and the stock. Season with salt and pepper and simmer for 5 minutes. Stir in the cornflour paste to thicken the sauce and simmer for another 1-2 minutes.

When sauce is almost finished, put the steaks in the preheated oven and roast for 5-7 minutes or until done to your liking. Allow to rest for 5 minutes before serving with a little hot mushroom sauce spooned over each. Place remaining sauce in a jug on the table. Serve with Potato Gratin with Gruyere and Garlic and Green Beans with Lemon.

Thai Style Beef Salad

You can serve this salad at room temperature, which is convenient when you're cooking for friends because you won't be rushing around at the last minute. To prepare it ahead of time, cut up the vegetables and herbs, cover and chill. Cook the meat about an hour before serving and combine all the ingredients just before serving.

Prep time   10 mins
Cook time   4-6 mins
              + 5 min resting
Serves   6

4-6 thick cut frying steaks
such as sirloin or rump
(about 150-200g per person)

splash of fish sauce

salt and ground black pepper

1 tbsp oil

3 Lebanese cucumbers
or 1 telegraph cucumber,
cut into small batons

1 small red onion,
halved and finely sliced

4 spring onions, thinly sliced

24 cherry tomatoes, halved

40 mint leaves, torn

4 tbsp coriander, chopped

⅔ cup Chilli Jam
(see page 128)

4 tbsp lime juice

Rub the steaks with the fish sauce and season them with salt and pepper. Heat the oil in a large frypan and cook the steaks for 2-3 minutes on each side or until they are done to your liking.

Rest the meat for at least 5 minutes after cooking before angle slicing thinly across the grain. If preparing the meat ahead of time, slice the steaks just before serving.

Place the sliced meat and any cooking juices in a mixing bowl with the prepared cucumber, red onion, spring onions, tomatoes, mint and coriander.

Mix together the Chilli Jam and lime juice, pour over the salad and toss to combine. If you want a side dish to serve with this, try plain rice or Green Bean and Peanut Noodles (see page 50).

Variation

If you don't have Chilli Jam in the fridge, you can substitute ⅔ cup sweet chilli sauce mixed with the finely grated zest of 2 limes and 2 tsp fish sauce.

Crispy Pork Belly

The key to great pork crackling is to dry the skin side of the meat well before sprinkling it with salt. Blast the pork in a hot oven to begin with to get the skin crunchy, then slow cook it for a further hour and a half in a bath of milk, which makes it really moist and tender. This is a very traditional Italian way to cook pork belly – one I learned from Elizabeth David's books.

Prep time	5 mins
Cook time	2 hours
Serves	6

1-1.2kg pork belly, skin scored

ground black pepper

1 tsp salt

2-3 sage leaves

2-2½ cups milk

To serve:
Crunchy New Potatoes
with Thyme
(see page 91)

Green Beans with Lemon
(see page 68)

Roasted Pepper Pesto
(see page 80)

Preheat oven to 240°C. Pat the skin of the meat dry and season the flesh side with pepper and half the salt. Sprinkle the sage leaves on the bottom of a metal baking dish (do not use a glass baking dish or it might shatter when you add the milk) and put the pork on top, skin side up. Season the top with the remaining salt.

Roast for 20-30 minutes at 240°C until the skin is starting to blister and crackle. Watch closely for burning.

Pour the milk around the meat to come about half to two thirds of the way up the sides of the pork. Reduce the heat to 160°C and roast for a further 1½ hours or until the meat is meltingly tender. Check the level of liquid during cooking and if it has evaporated add a little more to the pan.

Remove the pork from the oven, lift it out of the dish and allow it to cool. Discard the liquids, which break into curds.

For easy cutting, place the meat flesh side up on a chopping board and use a heavy, sharp knife to cut it into slices about 3-4cm thick. Serve warm or at room temperature with Crunchy New Potatoes with Thyme, Green Beans with Lemon, and Roasted Pepper Pesto.

Roast Pork with Fennel, Onions and Apples

Any dish that can be prepared in advance and left to take care of itself appeals to me. You could use any pork roast or even chicken (see below). If using a pork rack, ask your butcher to score the skin, trim or 'French' the rack and shorten the bones. Accompany with Creamy Polenta Bake (see page 105) and Braised Red Cabbage (see page 96).

Prep time   15 mins
Cook time   approx 2 hours
Serves   6-8

1 whole pork rack
(approx 2.5kg or 9-10 chops),
skin scored finely

1 tsp fennel seeds

salt and ground black pepper

2 red onions, peeled and cut
into thin wedges

2 apples or pears, cored and
sliced into thin wedges

1 head fennel, thinly sliced
(optional)

4-5 bay leaves

2 cups Verjuice
(see page 287)
or white wine

To serve:
Creamy Polenta Bake
(see page 105)

Preheat oven to 240°C. Pat the pork skin dry with a paper towel. Grind the fennel seeds and rub them into the exposed flesh (not the rind) of the pork. Season with salt and pepper.

Place the onion, apple or pear and fennel, if using, in a large roasting dish and top with the bay leaves. Place the pork on top, skin side up. Pour the Verjuice or wine around the pork, avoiding the skin of the pork as it needs to be dry to create crackling. If desired, wrap the exposed bones with tinfoil to prevent browning.

Roast at 240°C for 25 minutes until the pork skin begins to crackle, taking care it does not burn. Reduce the heat to 160°C and cook for another 1½ hours. Check occasionally, adding a little water to the dish if it looks like it's drying out. There should still be quite a lot of liquid at the end so you can spoon the juices over the meat to serve.

Remove the pork from the oven, remove the foil, if using, and stand the rack for about 5 minutes before carving. Slice between the bones to separate into cutlets. Serve on a bed of Creamy Polenta and the cooked onion, apple or pear and fennel from the roasting dish, with the juices spooned over the top.

Roast Chicken with Fennel, Onions and Apples

Prepare as for roast pork (see above), placing one or two whole chickens on top of the vegetables, pouring in the Verjuice (see page 287) and roasting at 200°C for 1 hour before reducing the heat to 180°C and cooking for a further 20-30 minutes. Serves 6-8.

Cypriot Shepherd's Pie

Shepherd's pie is one of those comforting dishes that adults and children both love. Here I've given it a Cypriot touch with the addition of cumin, cinnamon and ginger. It's the perfect dish to make mid-week, as it can be prepared ahead of time and then baked to golden perfection just before serving. If you prefer you can top it with mashed potato, but the parsnip carrot mash works so well with these flavours.

Prep time	20 mins
Cook time	approx 1 hour
Serves	4

3 tbsp oil

600g lean lamb mince

salt and ground black pepper

1 large onion, finely diced

2 garlic cloves, crushed

1 tbsp grated fresh ginger

2 tsp ground cumin

½ tsp ground cinnamon

2 tbsp tomato paste

1 large carrot, coarsely grated

400g can tomatoes

3 cups vegetable stock

1 tsp chopped rosemary

½ cup finely chopped parsley

1 recipe Parsnip
and Carrot Mash
(see page 96)

Heat half the oil in a large frypan over a high heat. Season the lamb with salt and pepper and fry in two batches until well browned. Set aside. Drain off any fat from the pan, add the remaining oil and cook the onion with the garlic, ginger, cumin and cinnamon over a medium heat until softened – about 6-7 minutes.

Add the tomato paste and stir over the heat for a minute or two. Add the browned lamb, carrot, tomatoes, stock and rosemary and simmer for about 30 minutes, stirring to loosen the pan brownings, until reduced to a thick, meaty sauce.

Mix in the parsley and adjust seasoning to taste. Transfer to a baking dish. Spread Parsnip and Carrot Mash over the lamb mixture. If not serving at once, cover and chill.

When ready to serve, preheat oven to 200°C and bake until mash is golden brown and filling is piping hot – about 30-40 minutes. Serve with steamed greens.

Braised Oxtails with Star Anise

This easy dish is sure to earn you compliments. Asian flavours blend with tomato and orange to give the oxtails a spicy kick and a rich, dark hue. It's one of those wonderful meals that require very little preparation and cook slowly until the meat is meltingly tender after a couple of hours. I often make it a day ahead to allow the flavours to develop. It freezes well. You can also use lamb shanks, or make it with browned stewing beef (use about 1.5kg cut into decent-sized chunks).

Prep time   10 mins
Cook time   3 hours
Serves   6

18-22 pieces (2-2.4kg) oxtail
or beef shin

salt and ground black pepper

2 cups tomato juice

2 cups water

1 tbsp brown sugar

2 tbsp rice wine vinegar

⅓ cup soy sauce

4 whole star anise

4 dried chillies

2 thumb-sized pieces fresh
ginger, thinly sliced (18 slices)

rind of ½ orange,
removed with a potato peeler
so there is no pith

1 whole head garlic, cloves
peeled, halved and trimmed

To serve:
Parsnip and Carrot Mash
(see page 96)

Gingered Bok Choy
(see page 102)

Pre-heat oven to 220°C and line a large roasting dish with baking paper for easy clean-up. Season the oxtails with salt and pepper and arrange in a single layer in the roasting dish. Roast for 30 minutes until well browned.

Remove oxtails from the roasting dish, discard fat and place oxtails into a lidded casserole dish. In a separate bowl, combine the tomato juice, water, sugar, vinegar and soy sauce. Scatter in the star anise, chillies, sliced ginger, orange rind and garlic cloves.

Pour the liquid over the browned meat, cover with a piece of baking paper to stop any exposed meat from drying out and cover the dish with a tight fitting lid. Turn the oven down to 180°C and cook for 2½ hours until very tender. This dish can be cooked a day or two ahead, in which case bake for 2 hours then reheat for 40 minutes at 180°C.

Serve with Parsnip and Carrot Mash and Gingered Bok Choy.

Lamb Racks with Salsa Verde

Lamb racks are not cheap to buy, so my aim with this recipe is to take all the risk out of cooking them. The most important thing to remember here is that your oven needs to be really hot before the lamb racks go in. It's also important to rest the meat for almost as long as you roast it. Covering it with tin foil and teatowels keeps it warm before carving and ensures an evenly cooked, moist result.

Prep time	20 mins
	+ marinating
Cook time	16-20 mins
	+ resting
Serves	6

3 lamb racks, trimmed,
or 6 lamb back straps
or 3-4 lamb rumps

4 tbsp Salsa Verde
(see page 60)

flaky salt and ground
black pepper

To serve:
Broad Bean Mash
with Mint and Parmesan
(see page 73)

extra Salsa Verde
(see page 60)

Rub the lamb all over with Salsa Verde and season with salt and pepper. Cover and stand for at least 30 minutes, or refrigerate for up to 12 hours. If you do put the lamb in the fridge, take it out 30 minutes before cooking so it can reach room temperature before going into the oven.

When you are ready to eat, preheat oven to 230°C. Transfer lamb to an oven tray or heavy cast iron dish and roast for 16-20 minutes or until it is done to your preference. Remove the dish from the oven, cover it with tinfoil and then place a couple of clean cloths over the top to keep it warm while it rests for 10-15 minutes.

Slice between the bones to separate the lamb rack into cutlets and serve on a bed of Broad Bean Mash with Mint and Parmesan, accompanied by an extra dish of Salsa Verde.

Asparagus, Snow Pea and Scallop
Salad with Citrus Chilli Dressing

∾

Lamb Racks with Salsa Verde

Broad Bean Mash
with Mint and Parmesan

Slow Roasted Red Onions

∾

Individual Berry Crumbles

from lake and sea

Wrested from the water,
glittering trophies of fish and seafood
are the ultimate gourmet treat.

It was our grandfather Put who first took us fishing when we were kids. He always seemed to know where the fish would be biting, and I can still recall the childhood triumphs of a safely landed catch. To this day it remains a simple thrill – bait a hook, drop a line and, with any luck, haul in dinner.

The excitement of pulling up a craypot and retrieving three enormous crayfish is just one of the many pleasures I discovered fishing in the spectacular fiords of New Zealand's southwestern coast. It's a breathtaking hour-long chopper ride over the mountains from Queenstown into Breaksea Sound. With no road access, this is one of the country's remotest areas and its pristine environment is almost otherworldly in its beauty.

As we ventured up Breaksea Sound, skipper and friend Greg Hay pulled out his chart revealing possies for scallops, cod, crayfish, paua and mussels, hapuku holes and, out on the coast, the runs yellow-fin tuna make in the autumn.

Given that this is one of the wettest places on earth, and ferocious storms lash in from Antarctica with unpredictable fury, the crystal blue skies and glassy sea we enjoyed were a rare gift. A resident pod of bottlenose dolphins cavorted nearby, flipping out of the water as if performing in an aquarium, running the bow line in a weaving dance, and showing off for the sheer joy of it.

The steep-sided fiords offer numerous sheltered anchorages, which have long attracted sailors and made Fiordland an area of early scientific discovery. Captain Cook put down in Dusky Sound for six weeks on his second trip to New Zealand in the autumn of 1773, charting the waters, replenishing supplies and collecting flora and fauna samples.

It would seem that little has changed in 230-odd years since Cook's visit. Certainly the whalers and sealers took their toll and fishing has diminished the seafood stocks, but the sheer remoteness of the Sounds means there are still fish aplenty.

While the world faces tremendous challenges of diminishing resources and a devastating loss of biodiversity, Fiordland remains a hideaway haven. The waters teem with life and you can find almost every seafood delicacy imaginable in plentiful supply, with 150 fish species known to exist here. I seemed to be very good at catching those bony little bait fish, before I managed to land a decent cod for our dinner.

Even the seal colonies that were annihilated by fur sealers at the end of the 18th century are coming back, and hopefully wise management of New Zealand's fishery resources will help reduce the risk of commercial overfishing and allow for a sustainable catch long into the future. For us recreational fisher folk, we need to land only what we can eat and be open to tasting something new, not just the well-loved favourites.

It would be great to think that our grandchildren and their grandchildren in turn may one day come here (and to other fishing spots around the globe) and marvel at the wilderness, taking the same pleasure in dropping a line and hauling in a wriggling fish for the table. When we shop we need to think about the fish we buy and choose species that are not endangered and that are being fished sustainably.

Prawn and Mint Finger Rolls

These look fancy, but they're remarkably easy and inexpensive. Adding lots of mint is the key to their zingy taste. The filling can also be served as a salad in its own right.

Prep time   30 mins
Serves   8-10

2 small bundles
(100g) bean thread
or rice vermicelli noodles

½ large iceberg lettuce

½ tsp sugar

1 large carrot,
peeled and coarsely grated

200g cooked prawn meat,
chopped

1 cup (60-70) mint leaves,
torn into pieces

3 tbsp chopped coriander

30 small or 20 large rounds
rice paper

To garnish:
½ cup roasted peanuts,
chopped (optional)

Place the noodles in a bowl, cover with boiling water and soak for 5 minutes. Drain the water off and then cut the noodles with kitchen scissors in several places to create shorter lengths.

Very finely shred the lettuce and place in a mixing bowl with sugar, carrot, prawn meat, mint and coriander. Mix through the noodles.

Dampen a clean teatowel and lay it on the bench. Dunk the rice paper rounds into a dish of warm water one at a time for a couple of seconds each (don't soak them or they will become too sticky), then place them separately on the damp teatowel. Wait for a minute for the rice paper to soften and become flexible. They are ready to work with when they are dimpled and softened. If you try to roll them before this they will split.

Place a small handful of the prawn mixture in the centre of each wrapper. Wet your hands to stop them sticking to the rice paper and then roll the wrapper up tightly around the filling, tucking in the sides as you go. Transfer the rolls to a plate, seam side down, and cover with a damp paper towel. If not serving immediately, they will hold their shape in the fridge for 24 hours. Garnish with chopped peanuts, if using, and serve with Chilli Lime Dipping Sauce (see below).

Variations

Omit the prawns and substitute 2 Lebanese cucumbers, deseeded and cut into thick matchsticks, and 1 cup bean sprouts. Or omit the prawns and use 200g shredded cooked chicken instead.

Chilli Lime Dipping Sauce

Place 2 cups sweet chilli sauce, the juice and finely grated zest of 4 limes, 3 tsp fish sauce and the white part of 1 spring onion, very finely chopped, in a jar and shake to combine. This sauce can be kept in the fridge for up to 4 weeks. Makes 2½ cups.

Spicy Casbah Prawns

This is another of those super quick, fabulously tasty dishes you can make with my Chermoula Dipping Sauce (see page 144). It's great with any seafood.

Prep time	5 mins
Cook time	2 mins
Serves	4 as an entrée or 2 as a main

18-24 large raw prawn tails, shells removed

salt and ground black pepper

1 tbsp extra virgin olive oil

1 cup Chermoula Dipping Sauce (see page 144)

To serve:
2 tbsp chopped coriander

wedges of fresh lime

Season the prawns with salt and pepper. Heat the oil in a large frypan and cook the prawns over a high heat until they turn pink – about 2 minutes. Add the Chermoula Dipping Sauce to the pan and sizzle for a minute. Serve immediately, garnished with coriander and with lime wedges on the side.

Crayfish Caesar Salad

❧

Barbecued Whole Fish
with Chilli Lime Salt
Buttered Wholegrain Bread

❧

Grilled Summer Fruit and Figs
with Port Wine Syrup
Chocolate and Cranberry Slice

Whitebait Fritters

Some people put flour in their whitebait fritters but I prefer this lighter version made without flour – it allows the subtle taste of the whitebait to shine through. Adding a bit of lemon juice brings out the seafood flavour.

Prep time	5 mins
Cook time	3-4 mins each
Makes	24 small fritters

2 eggs

200g whitebait

1 tbsp lemon juice

salt and ground black pepper, to taste

To cook:
a little butter

To serve:
lemon wedges
Horseradish Cream
(see below)

Lightly whisk eggs in a mixing bowl. Add whitebait, lemon juice and salt and pepper and stir to combine.

Melt a knob of butter in a heavy-based frypan over a hot heat. When the butter is sizzling and almost nut brown, drop small spoonfuls of the mixture into the pan. Cook for 1-2 minutes on each side, or until egg has set and fritters are lightly golden.

Repeat with further batches, buttering the pan between batches, until all mixture has been used. Serve warm or at room temperature with lemon wedges and a dish of Horseradish Cream.

Horseradish Cream

This makes a delicious dipping sauce to serve with any seafood. Mix together in a bowl 1 cup light sour cream, 2 tbsp horseradish, 1 tsp lemon juice, 2 tbsp chopped capers and 1 tbsp finely chopped dill, chervil or parsley. Season to taste with a little salt and ground black pepper. Sauce will keep in a covered container in the fridge for about a week. Makes 1¼ cups.

In search of white gold

There is more than a thread of commonality between the occupations of whitebaiting and gold mining. Both require a huge sense of optimism, no concern for inclement weather, and the preparedness to rough it in the wilderness for the chance of a lucky strike. The moniker 'white gold' is given to whitebait, thanks to the hefty price tag and silvery colour of these tiny fish.

The visceral sense of anticipation, the thrill of landing a run, the pristine beauty of the great outdoors, and the pioneering notion that with nothing more than a net and some luck on your side you might make a fortune, lure a breed of people to fish the waterways of New Zealand for three months each year. Their prize is the tiny transparent whitebait that run in shoals upstream each spring to spawn.

For the last day of the whitebaiting season I joined 'baiters' Charlie and Carol Boulton on the west coast of the South Island. There had been few big catches at Haast throughout the season (not that any 'baiter' will ever let on if he or she has hit the jackpot), but those in the game fish from dawn to dusk, rain or shine, pretty much every day regardless.

For us Kiwis, whitebait sits right up there as the ultimate delicacy, an iconic part of our heritage for which we are prepared to part with big money. While whitebait fisheries also exist in Chile, Argentina, North America, China, Japan, Holland, North Africa and the Philippines, they are small by comparison to ours. It is only here in New Zealand that the whitebait season is an integral part of the calendar, approached with such a pioneering passion.

There are five Galaxiid species, the most common here being the inanga (G.maculatus). All are about the length of your little finger, and have a clean, delicate flavour. People who eat a lot of whitebait will tell you that the slightly milkier species known as Kaora (G. brevipinnis) has more flavour, but whatever the species whitebait are a taste that, once discovered, becomes a food lover's obsession.

Twice Baked Whitebait Soufflés

This double baking technique is an exception to the rule that soufflés must be served at once. The mixture is baked and will then hold for up to two days in the refrigerator before being baked a second time with a topping of cream, which makes it puff up again. Most recipes for double baked soufflés call for them to be turned out of the dishes for the second baking, but I find it works just as well to leave them in the dishes.

Prep time	15 mins
Cook time	15-20 mins for first baking + 12-15 mins for second stage
Serves	6

50g butter, plus extra to butter ramekins or cups

½ cup flour

1¾ cups milk

pinch of freshly ground nutmeg

1 tsp salt

generous shake of white pepper

finely grated zest of 1 lemon

4 tbsp lemon juice

5 egg yolks

1 cup whitebait
or 1 cup finely chopped smoked salmon

2 tbsp finely chopped soft herbs such as chervil, basil or parsley

5 egg whites

To finish:
6 tbsp cream

Preheat oven to 180°C. Generously butter six 1 cup ramekins and put them in the fridge to chill.

In a medium saucepan, melt the butter until sizzling but not browned. Stir in the flour and cook, stirring, for about 2 minutes until the mixture forms a smooth paste. Whisk in the milk, nutmeg, salt and pepper and lemon zest and bring back to a boil, stirring constantly, until the sauce thickens (it will be very thick).

Add lemon juice and whisk until smooth. Remove from heat and beat in egg yolks one at a time. Taste for seasoning – it should taste highly seasoned. Fold through whitebait or smoked salmon and herbs.

Place egg whites in a clean, dry bowl and beat until they form soft peaks. Add one quarter of the egg whites to the whitebait mixture and stir until well mixed. Then fold the remaining egg whites gently through the mixture.

Fill the buttered ramekins to the top, then run your thumb around the inside edge of the dishes so the soufflés puff evenly. Set the ramekins in a deep roasting dish and pour boiling water around them until it comes about halfway up the sides of the dishes. This water bath will help the soufflés cook evenly. Bake until they are lightly puffed, browned and just set in the centre – about 15-20 minutes. (The soufflés can be cooked right through at this point if you prefer. Cook for about 20-25 minutes total.)

Remove the soufflés from the oven and the water bath and leave to cool. They can be covered and refrigerated for up to 2 days. When you are ready to serve them, preheat oven to 220°C. Pour 1 tbsp of cream over each soufflé. Place on a tray and cook until they are risen, crusty and golden – about 12-15 minutes from refrigerated.

We all share in the desire
for a healthy life and a food
chain we can trust.

Tea Smoked Salmon or Trout

The flavour of home smoked seafood is exceptional and it is so easy to prepare. If you are smoking food inside, you will need either a heavy wok or a deep roasting dish, plus a rack that fits inside it and a tight-fitting lid. I like to use lapsang souchong or caravan tealeaves because of their smoky flavour, but you could use English breakfast tea or even untreated sawdust instead. You can also use this method to smoke mussels, tomatoes, garlic or salt.

Prep time	15 mins + 10 mins standing time
Cook time	20 mins + 15 mins standing time
Serves	6-8

2 tbsp scotch whisky
or water

1 tbsp brown sugar

1 tsp salt

1 side of salmon or trout,
skin on

To smoke:
3 tsp tealeaves
or 2 tbsp untreated sawdust

1 tsp sugar

To serve:
1 cup Horseradish Cream
(see page 181)

1 Crusty Flat Bread
(see page 18)

Mix scotch whisky or water with sugar and salt. Rub over the flesh side of the fish and leave to stand for 10 minutes before smoking (or up to 2 hours in the fridge, flesh side down in the whisky mixture).

Line a wok or roasting dish with enough foil to reach 3-4 cm above the rim, flattening the foil firmly on the base and sides. Sprinkle the tealeaves or sawdust and sugar in the base. Position an oiled rack above the tealeaves and place the fish skin side down on the rack. Make sure there is enough room above the fish for the air to circulate and smoke the fish thoroughly.

Cover the wok or roasting dish tightly with a lid and fold the overhanging foil in and around the edge of the lid to seal. Place wok or roasting dish on the stove top over a high heat for 4-6 minutes (by this stage the mixture should be smoking vigorously), then reduce to a low heat and cook for a further 12 minutes. Turn off the heat but keep the lid closed for another 15 minutes so the fish absorbs the smoky flavours while it cools.

Before serving, remove the pin bones from the cooked fish with a clean pair of tweezers or small pliers. Grasp one bone at a time and pull out in the direction the bone is lying.

Transfer fish to a serving platter and serve with Horseradish Cream and Crusty Flat Bread.

Prawn and Coriander Spring Rolls

You can buy commercially prepared spring rolls but it's so much healthier and more satisfying to make your own and bake, rather than fry, them. You can substitute fish or chicken instead of prawn meat in this recipe.

Prep time	20 mins
Cook time	20 mins
Makes	18

100g rice vermicelli
or bean thread noodles

300g raw prawn meat
or fish or chicken

2 tbsp sweet chilli sauce

4 tbsp chopped coriander

1 tbsp fish sauce

1 tbsp finely grated ginger

green part of 1 spring onion,
finely chopped

1 egg white

18 spring roll wrappers

approx 4 tbsp oil

To serve:
1 recipe Lemongrass
and Chilli Dipping Sauce
(see below)

Pour boiling water over the noodles and leave to soften for about 5 minutes. Drain thoroughly, shaking out any excess water.

Finely chop prawns, fish or chicken. Combine with drained noodles, sweet chilli sauce, coriander, fish sauce, ginger, spring onion and egg white in a bowl. Mix until evenly combined.

Place 2 tbsp of mixture in the centre of each spring roll wrapper, fold in ends and roll up tightly like a fat cigar. Place on a baking tray lined with baking paper and chill until ready to cook – up to 4 hours.

Preheat oven to 200°C. Brush spring rolls with oil and bake until golden and crisp – about 20 minutes. Serve with Lemongrass and Chilli Dipping Sauce.

Lemongrass and Chilli Dipping Sauce

Combine 3 tsp finely grated lemongrass, ½ cup sweet chilli sauce, ¼ cup water, 2 tbsp fish sauce, 2 finely chopped kaffir lime leaves or the finely grated zest of 1 lime, 2 tbsp lime juice, 2 cloves crushed garlic and 2 tsp minced fresh ginger. This sauce keeps for weeks in the fridge. Makes 1 cup.

Crayfish Caesar Salad

Here's my upmarket adaptation of the classic Caesar Salad recipe. If you can't source fresh crayfish, prawns make a fine substitute. To dispatch your crayfish humanely, put them in the freezer for at least 30 minutes.

Prep time	10 mins
Serves	6

2-3 freshly cooked crayfish tails
or 1-1.2kg prawn tails

2 large heads romaine
or cos lettuce,
leaves washed and dried

3 big handfuls (100g)
Oven Baked Croutons
(see page 211)
or bought bagel crisps

50g shaved parmesan

1 recipe Creamy Seafood
Dressing (see below)

If you're using crayfish tails, remove the cooked flesh from the shells and cut it into chunks. If you're using prawn tails, boil them in salted water, then peel and devein them.

When you're ready to serve the salad, slice the lettuce leaves into 3-4cm wide slices. Cut or break the croutons or bagel crisps into pieces and place in a large serving bowl with lettuce, parmesan and crayfish or prawns. Add Creamy Seafood Dressing and toss to combine. Serve at once.

Creamy Seafood Dressing

Heat 1 tbsp olive oil in a small frypan. Add 2 cloves crushed garlic and 4-5 canned anchovies and cook over a medium heat for 1 minute, mashing the anchovies to a paste. Add 1 cup cream, ½ cup finely grated parmesan and ground black pepper. Boil hard for 2 minutes until bubbles start to get big, which shows the sauce is thickening. Cool before using. This is a great dressing for any kind of seafood. Makes 1 cup.

Herb Fritters with Smoked Salmon

If you're making fritters in bulk, you can speed up the process by quickly browning them and then finishing them in an 180°C oven for 8-10 minutes until spongy to the touch.

Prep time	5 mins + 15 mins standing time
Cook time	4-5 mins per batch
Makes	60 small or 30 medium fritters

1½ cups plain flour

3 tsp baking powder

3 eggs

1 cup soda water or water, chilled

1 tsp salt

ground black pepper

½ cup finely chopped basil

finely grated zest of 1 lemon

2-3 tbsp neutral oil or spray oil

To serve:
150g thinly sliced smoked salmon

½ cup sour cream and sprigs of dill

To make the fritter base batter, combine the flour, baking powder, eggs, soda water or water (the soda water makes the fritters particularly light), salt and pepper in a mixing bowl, beating to make a smooth batter. Cover and stand for 15 minutes or for up to 4 hours in the fridge (this allows the gluten in the flour to rest and ensures the fritters will be tender). This base batter can be flavoured with different ingredients (see below).

Stir chopped herbs and lemon zest into the rested batter.
Heat a heavy frypan over a medium heat and coat or spray lightly with the oil. Drop small spoonfuls of mixture into the hot pan and cook until bubbles form in the mixture, then turn to cook the other side. Fritters are cooked when they bounce back when pressed gently. Lightly re-oil pan between batches.

Top each fritter with a small slice of smoked salmon and garnish with a little sour cream and a sprig of dill.

Zucchini, Feta and Mint Fritters

Grate 2 medium zucchini (about 300g) onto a clean teatowel, gather up and twist to squeeze out the moisture. Place zucchini in a bowl and stir in finely grated zest of 1 lemon, 1 tbsp lemon juice, 2 tbsp finely chopped spring onions (green part only), ¼ cup chopped mint leaves and 150g finely crumbled feta. Stir into the rested fritter batter (see above). Cook as above. Makes 30 medium or 60 small fritters.

Corn Fritters

Mix 3 cups corn kernels, ½ cup grated mozzarella or cheddar cheese and 1 tbsp pesto (optional) into the rested fritter batter (see above). Cook as above. Serves 4.

Asparagus, Snow Pea and Scallop Salad

This impressive salad makes a few scallops go a long way, but you can replace them with seared prawns or even six rashers of bacon that have been cooked until crisp and then crumbled. If it's not asparagus season simply double the amount of snow peas. It's a perfect dish for when you want to be organised. The asparagus and snow peas can be cooked a couple of hours before you eat, the scallops seared up to half an hour ahead of serving and the Citrus Chilli Dressing will keep for up to a week in the fridge.

Prep time   5 mins
Cook time   5-7 mins
Serves   6

24 spears fresh asparagus, tough ends snapped off

3 handfuls (100g) snow peas, trimmed of stringy bits

2 handfuls (50g) rocket leaves

flesh of 1 large just-ripe avocado, cut into chunks

24 fresh scallops (or more as extravagance allows)

finely grated zest of ½ lemon or lime

salt and ground black pepper

a pinch of sugar

2 tbsp extra virgin olive oil

¼ cup Citrus Chilli Dressing (see below)

Bring a large pot of water to the boil. Lightly salt the water then drop in the trimmed asparagus and return to the boil for 3 minutes. Add the snow peas to the pot for the final 20 seconds of the cooking time. Do not overcook.

Drain then immediately cover the vegetables with cold water (this helps to capture their vivid green colour and crunchiness). Drain the vegetables thoroughly. Arrange the rocket leaves on a serving platter and place the asparagus and snow peas on top. Top with the avocado chunks.

Mix the scallops with the lemon or lime zest and season with salt, pepper and sugar (the sugar helps the scallops caramelise without overcooking). Heat the olive oil in a heavy-based frypan until it is very hot and cook the scallops for about 30-50 seconds on each side – they should be browned but still soft. Don't overcook them and don't overcrowd the pan – you may need to sear them in two batches.

Pile scallops on top of salad, drizzle with ¼ cup Citrus Chilli Dressing and toss. Divide between 6 serving plates and serve at once.

Citrus Chilli Dressing

Place ¼ cup each of orange, lime and lemon juice in a large jar with 1 tsp rice vinegar, 1 tbsp fish sauce, 1 tbsp sugar, ground black pepper and 1 small red chilli, seeds removed and flesh very finely diced. Shake to blend and chill until ready to serve. This dressing is great with seafood, chicken or salad greens and keeps for up to a week in the fridge. Makes ½ cup.

In the rhythm of the day, it's great to find a moment when things can happen at their own easy pace.

Asian Prawn and Noodle Salad

This is one of those super easy, toss-together salads. With a packet of prawns or shrimps in the freezer it makes a perfect dish to serve when friends turn up unexpectedly.

Prep time   10 mins
Serves   2 as a main,
            4 as a starter

250g rice stick noodles

250g prawns or shrimps, peeled and deveined

1 tsp grapeseed, rice bran or other neutral oil

1 tbsp finely grated ginger

2 spring onions, finely sliced

2 tbsp chopped fresh coriander

½ cup roasted peanuts, chopped

1 recipe Lemongrass and Chilli Dipping Sauce (see page 190)

Drop the rice noodles into a large pot of boiling water. Remove the pot from the heat immediately and allow to stand and cool for 10 minutes or longer. Drain the noodles then rinse under cold water.

If the prawns or shrimps are frozen, thaw them then pat dry with a paper towel. Heat the oil in a frypan and sauté the prawns or shrimps with the ginger over a medium heat until they are cooked through. Place in a serving bowl with the cooked noodles, spring onions, chopped coriander, peanuts and Lemongrass and Chilli Dipping Sauce. Toss and serve.

This salad can be made up to 2 hours before serving. Toss again just before serving.

Fire Baked Salmon or Trout

This is a genius way of cooking freshly caught fish. I've only done it with lake-caught fish but I'm sure it would be equally fabulous with fresh fish from the sea. It's as easy as wrapping the whole fish in paper, soaking it in water and then burying the lot in the embers of a fire. You can cook it on a wood fire or barbecue, or even in the oven – you won't get the same smoky flavour in the oven, but you'll still get extremely succulent fish.

Prep time   5 mins
Cook time   20-40 mins
Serves   3-4

2-3kg fresh whole salmon or trout, cleaned

fresh mint, dill or coriander sprigs

salt and pepper

To wrap:
3 sheets white butcher's paper or parchment

8 sheets newspaper

To serve:
lemon wedges

Crusty Flat Bread
(see page 18)

Salsa Verde
(see page 60)

Horseradish Cream
(see page 181)

Light a fire in a fire pit, barbecue or pizza oven and allow it to settle to a bed of hot embers.

In the meantime, stuff the cleaned fish cavity with the mint, dill or coriander sprigs and season the fish inside and out with salt and pepper. Place it on 3 large sheets of butcher's paper or parchment and wrap up to enclose the fish tightly. Stack 8 sheets of newspaper, place the wrapped fish on top and wrap it up tightly to make a parcel that won't easily fall apart.

Dunk the parcel in water to thoroughly wet the paper. Place the parcel on the bed of embers and cook for 30-40 minutes, turning every 10 minutes. The cooking time will depend on the size of your fish and the heat of your embers. Check whether the fish is ready by inserting a sharp skewer just below the gills in the thick part of the back. When the fish is done you should feel no resistance.

To oven bake your fish, preheat the oven to 200°C. Place the wet wrapped fish in the hot oven and cook for 20-30 minutes. Test for doneness as above.

Once the fish is cooked, remove the parcel from the fire or oven and cool enough so that you can safely unwrap it. Peel off the charred paper and then the fish skin. Transfer to a serving platter and serve accompanied by lemon wedges and Crusty Flat Bread. It's also delicious with my Salsa Verde or Horseradish Cream.

Five Spice Salt and Pepper Squid

Squid goes from being tender and delicious to boot leather tough in a short space of cooking time. The trick is to cook it fast – that way you can guarantee tenderness. You can serve it hot as it comes from the pan or at room temperature. Surprisingly it reheats well in a hot oven without going soggy – the key is to drain it in a single layer.

Prep time	15 mins
Cook time	1-1½ mins per batch
Serves	6 as a starter

3 large (500g) squid tubes, cleaned

1 cup rice flour

½ tsp five spice powder

1 tsp salt

1 tsp ground black pepper

To fry:
grapeseed or other neutral oil

To serve:
6 handfuls (150g) watercress sprigs or rocket leaves

juice of 1 lemon

1 cup Roasted Garlic Aioli (see page 56)

lemon wedges

Cut the squid tubes into rings about finger thickness. If there are any tentacles, separate them into individual pieces.

In a bowl combine the rice flour, five spice powder, salt and pepper. Toss the squid in the flour mixture to coat. Discard excess flour.

Pour neutral oil to 4cm depth in a medium saucepan and heat to 180°C. Test the oil temperature with a cube of bread – it should turn golden brown in 30 seconds. If the oil is too hot add a little cold oil.

Add the coated squid a handful at a time. Don't overcrowd the pan. Cook each batch for 1-1½ minutes until crispy and golden – don't overcook it or it will be rubbery! Lift the squid out of the oil with a slotted spoon and shake it to remove the excess oil. Set aside on paper towels. Continue cooking, making sure that the cooked squid is drained in a single layer on paper towels – don't stack it up or it will steam and go soggy.

The cooked squid can be served hot or at room temperature. If you want to make it ahead and serve it hot, simply arrange it in a single layer on an oven tray and reheat in a 220°C oven for 3-4 minutes.

To serve, place a handful of watercress or rocket on each plate, top with squid, squeeze a little fresh lemon juice over the top and drizzle with Roasted Garlic Aioli. Serve garnished with lemon wedges, with extra aioli in a bowl on the side.

Steamed Mussels with Creamy Harvest Sauce

This works well as a lunch or light dinner with lots of crusty bread to mop up the juices.

Prep time	5 mins
Cook time	6-8 mins
Serves	2

24 fresh mussels

1 cup Harvest Tomato Sauce
(see page 62)
or 1 cup tomato pasta sauce

½ cup cream

To serve:
2 tbsp chopped Italian parsley

crusty bread

Scrub the mussels and remove their beards. Bring ¼ cup water to a boil in a large pot. Add mussels, replace the lid and steam mussels until they open – about 3-4 minutes. Discard any that won't close when you tap them or don't open after this amount of cooking.

Drain mussels in a colander and return to the pot. Add Harvest Tomato Sauce and cream. Bring to a boil then take off the heat so the seafood does not overcook. Pile into deep serving bowls, sprinkle with parsley and accompany with crusty bread to mop up the sauce.

Whole Baked Fish Flavoured with Curry Base

Spread South East Asian Curry Base (see page 112) over a whole fish and bake for 30-40 minutes to create a dramatic and succulent centrepiece to an Asian themed meal.

Prep time	5 mins
Cook time	30-40 mins
Serves	2-4 as part of a shared meal

1-1.5kg whole fish
such as snapper or sea bass,
cleaned and scaled

½ cup South East Asian Curry
Base (see page 112)

To serve:
plain steamed rice

lightly cooked green vegetables

Preheat oven to 180°C. Cut 3 slashes on each side of the fish. Rub the curry base on both sides of the fish and rub a little inside the cavity.

Place the fish in an ovenproof dish and bake for 30-40 minutes until it is just cooked through. Serve with plain steamed rice and lightly cooked green vegetables.

Barbecued Whole Fish with Chilli Lime Salt

There's no better way to cook or eat fish than barbecued straight from the sea. It makes dinner not just a meal but a shared taste experience. If you're buying, rather than catching, your fish, use your eyes and your nose. Really fresh fish smells of the sea – nothing fishy. Eyeball it for bright eyes and firm, glistening flesh.

Prep time   10 mins
Cook time   15 mins
Serves   4

2-3kg whole fish, head removed and gutted but with skin and scales left on

3 tbsp butter

2 tsp Chilli Lime Salt (see page 78) or plain sea salt

To serve:
wedges of lemon or lime

buttered wholegrain bread

Cut the fish along the backbone without cutting right through and open it out flat (or have your fishmonger do this for you). Spread the inside flesh liberally with butter and sprinkle with Chilli Lime Salt or sea salt.

Place the fish skin side down on a preheated barbecue and cook, uncovered, until the butter starts to melt and the flesh starts to turn white 2cm in from the sides at the widest part. This will take about 10 minutes. At this point cover the fish and cook for 5-6 minutes longer. To check whether it is cooked through poke the thickest part of the fish with a skewer. The flesh should flake.

Slide the fish onto a platter and stand for 5 minutes before serving. Lift out the bones and discard. Serve accompanied by wedges of lemon or lime and buttered wholegrain bread.

Spicy Garlic Paste

This is a classic accompaniment to traditional French seafood soups like my Fragrant Seafood Bowl (see page 212). It was taught to me by my dear friend, fabulous French cook Danièle Delpeuch, and differs from many similar recipes in that it uses mashed potato as a base instead of mayonnaise. Spread it onto Oven Baked Croutons (see below) and then dunk or float them in the soup. You can also serve it as a dip with slices of soft French bread.

Prep time	10 mins
Makes	approx 1½ cups

6 cloves garlic,
peeled and chopped

1 tsp salt

1 large potato,
boiled and mashed

1-2 tsp minced chillies, to taste
(it should be quite fiery)

1 egg yolk

¼ tsp paprika
or smoked paprika

1 tsp dried espelette pepper
or hot paprika (optional)

½ cup extra virgin olive oil

Crush the garlic and salt together on a chopping board with the back of a knife to form a paste. Stir it into the mashed potato with the minced chillies, egg yolk, paprika and espelette pepper or hot paprika, if using. Stir in the oil to form a spreadable paste. Stored in a jar in the fridge, Spicy Garlic Paste will keep for 2-3 days.

Oven Baked Croutons

Preheat oven to 180°C. Cut a French stick or country bread loaf on an angle into 2cm thick slices. Brush or spray both sides of each slice with a little extra virgin olive oil and spread onto an oven tray in a single layer. Bake for about 15 minutes until golden brown and crisp. Keep an eye on the bread as it can darken and burn quickly. Allow to cool. Croutons will keep for a couple of weeks if stored in an airtight container.

Fragrant Seafood Bowl

This soup tastes better if you use 2-3 different kinds of fish. Prawns or mussels are a great addition too. In France, this dish is usually served with Oven Baked Croutons topped with Spicy Garlic Paste (see page 211), and to me this is what makes it special.

Prep time   20 mins
Cook time   60 mins
Serves   8

½ cup extra virgin olive oil

1 onion, finely chopped

1 fennel bulb, thinly sliced

2 small leeks, thinly sliced

2 tbsp tomato paste

2-3 bay leaves

4 large garlic cloves, minced

1-2 red chillies, to taste

½ cup vermouth

big pinch (20-30) saffron threads

2 x 400g cans tomatoes in juice, chopped, or 800g fresh tomatoes, peeled and chopped

1 tsp honey

8 cups fish stock

5 medium potatoes, peeled and cut into 2cm chunks

salt and ground black pepper

1kg boneless fillets of firm fish

12-16 mussels and/or 8-16 large raw prawns (optional)

To serve:
1 recipe each Spicy Garlic Paste and Oven Baked Croutons (see page 211)

Heat the oil in a large pot and sweat the onion, fennel and leeks for about 15-20 minutes until the vegetables are clear and softened. Do not allow them to brown.

Add tomato paste and sizzle for a couple of minutes. Add bay leaves, garlic and whole chillies. Mix in vermouth, saffron, tomatoes and honey and cook for 20 minutes over a low heat.

Add the fish stock and potatoes and bring back to a simmer. Simmer for 10-15 minutes until the potatoes are nearly cooked. Season with salt and pepper to taste.

Cut fish into 4cm chunks. Five minutes before serving, add fish and mussels, if using, and simmer for 3-4 minutes. Then add prawns, if using, and simmer for another 2-3 minutes until the seafood is cooked and the mussels open. Discard any mussels that don't open.

Lift out and discard bay leaves and chillies. Divide soup between heated soup bowls. Spread Spicy Garlic Paste on Oven Baked Croutons and float them in the soup to serve.

When nature provides us with such
wonderful resources, it seems only
right to enjoy them.

from the larder

With their seductive richness, the offerings of the dairy bring indulgence to the table.

When I started cooking it all seemed so easy. Simply by adding buckets of cream, butter or oil to a dish it would taste utterly seductive – wickedly, devastatingly irresistible. It took me some time to work out that you only need a smidge of fat. Use too much and your fresh ingredients are overwhelmed, their essential tastes masked in a dull, cloying richness.

When I was 19, I was offered a job cooking in a little restaurant, finding myself behind the stove whipping up cream-laden plates of tender veal and sage rolls, buttery ravioli and unctuous rich, smooth soups with killer calories. I churned out litre upon litre of the world's best ice cream, and rolled round upon round of creamy chocolate truffles (the recipes for these two sweet indulgences can be found in the pages that follow – both are too good to leave out).

Along the way I piled on the kilos, oblivious to the fact that it was all the fat I was using that was turning me into a replica of the Michelin man. These days I have learnt that you can make great tasting food without relying on lots of fat to deliver flavour.

Without a doubt, a judicious dollop of cream or butter is one of the quickest ways to create a little luxury on the plate, adding a richness and lip-smacking mouth-feel to many a dish. But with a good pantry – a toolkit of flavour notes – you can create interesting tastes without needing much fat.

Ginger, garlic and onions provide base notes, the juice and zest of lemons and limes deliver bright freshness, fresh herbs lend another clean, vibrant flavour hit, fresh spices add nuance, and stocks and Asian sauces like fish sauce, soy or tamari provide a depth of flavour.

Some dishes demand lashings of cream or butter
to taste as they are meant to taste – ice cream as
ice cream, chocolate ganache as chocolate ganache.
There's no point trying to cut back here – you'll just
be disappointed.

From a litre of milk, a mere two or three tablespoons
of cream will settle to the top. Churn this cream
and you get half its weight in butter. Through this
process of distillation, the richness condenses into
dense, hard fat. You need 10 litres of milk to yield
a kilo of cheese – a ratio of 10 to one. I never cease
to be amazed that, be it a nutty, slightly granular
Parmesan or a buttery, tangy blue, each type of
cheese is simply a different expression of milk.
By changing the temperature it is made at, the time
it takes to mature and the type of culture used, you
end up with a different cheese.

I confess to an absolute weakness for cheese.
My tastebuds light up for a melting, mushroomy brie
or the lightly acidic tang of a creamy soft goat curd.
When I was pregnant with our daughter Rose I found
myself obsessed by a craving for pungently aromatic
taleggio. This stinkiest of washed rind cheeses hails
from Lombardy in north Italy. I just could not get
enough of that smooth, velvety texture, the funky
mouth-filling taste and sticky red rind. Ahhh, what
pure pleasure...

The greatest enemy of cheese is air. For this reason
it's best to buy larger pieces of cheese and store
them in a cool place with the cut edges protected
with waxed paper so they won't dry out. For cooking
I always like to keep a block of parmesan (or the
less expensive grana padano) in the fridge, along
with feta and gruyere or a sharp cheddar. These
cheeses, along with other dairy staples of yoghurt,
milk, butter and cream, give you the scope to create
dishes that are silky smooth and richly satisfying.

Soft Fresh Cheese

There is something wonderfully satisfying about making your own cheese and this is such a simple recipe, yielding a creamy, tangy soft cheese. Start preparing it the day before you want to serve it. It will keep for over a week in the fridge.

| Prep time | 10 mins
+ draining
overnight |
| Makes | 2 cups |

1kg Greek, goat milk or buffalo milk yoghurt, unsweetened

1½ tsp salt

Mix the yoghurt with the salt. Line a sieve with paper towels or clean muslin, add the salted yoghurt and place the sieve over a bowl to drain. Place it in the fridge or a cool place overnight.

In the morning, discard the liquid produced and turn the cheese out of the sieve into a bowl. Soft Fresh Cheese keeps in a covered container in the fridge for about a week.

Herbed Fresh Cheese

Make Soft Fresh Cheese as above. Turn the cheese out into a bowl and stir in 2 tbsp finely chopped basil, 1 tbsp chopped chives and 1 tsp finely chopped rosemary. Makes 2 cups.

Sweet Fresh Cheese

For a sweet dessert cheese plate, prepare the Soft Fresh Cheese as above. Turn the cheese out into a bowl and mix in 2 tbsp liquid honey or icing sugar and 1 tsp ground cardamom or cinnamon. Stir to thoroughly combine. When ready to serve, divide between 6 plates and garnish each plate with 2 fresh dates, pear slices and a drizzle of honey. Serves 6.

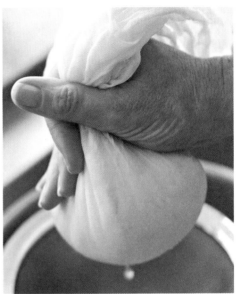

Crème Fraîche

Crème fraîche means fresh cream in French, but in fact this is the most luxurious of sour creams. It is expensive to buy but really easy and fun to make at home.

Prep time	5 mins + 48 hours resting

2 cups cream

3 tbsp buttermilk

Heat cream until just tepid (you just want to take the chill off it). Remove from heat and stir in buttermilk. Put in a lidded glass jar and leave to rest at room temperature for 24 hours, stirring a couple of times. Don't worry about leaving the mixture out of the fridge, as the cultures in the buttermilk stop it from going off and will transform the mixture into Crème Fraîche.

After 24 hours at room temperature the mixture will have thickened somewhat. Stir or shake, cover again and put in the fridge for another 24 hours. It will continue to thicken a little and will develop the lovely light acidic flavour that defines Crème Fraîche. To thicken, simply shake in the jar or whip to your desired consistency. Crème Fraîche will keep in the fridge for up to 10 days.

Crème Anglaise

This light vanilla custard sauce adds an elegant flourish to desserts like my Baked Apples (see page 285). Purists don't add any cornflour but I find it helps to ensure a thick, velvety custard. For a thicker custard, use an extra teaspoon of cornflour.

Prep time	15 mins
Cook time	5 mins
Makes	2 cups

2 cups milk

¼ cup sugar

3 egg yolks

2 tsp cornflour

1 tsp vanilla extract

5 cardamom pods (optional)

Heat the milk in a pot. While it is heating, put the sugar, egg yolks and cornflour in a bowl and whisk to combine.

Mix a little of the hot milk into the egg yolk mixture, then stir the egg mixture into the remaining hot milk. Add vanilla and cardamom pods, if using. Stir over a low heat until thickened slightly, then allow to simmer for another 40-50 seconds, stirring gently.

If you're not using the Crème Anglaise at once, cover the surface with waxed paper to prevent a skin forming. (It will keep in a covered container in the fridge for a week.) Gently reheat when required.

Pistachio and Berry Ice Cream

If you've never made ice cream before, this recipe is the one to try. All you need is three bowls and an electric beater. My mother made this ice cream throughout my childhood and I've continued the tradition with my own children. The Ice Cream Base recipe can be flavoured with chocolate or jam (see page 229), or for a special occasion make this wonderful pistachio and berry mixture.

Prep time	20 mins + at least 4 hours freezing time
Makes	2.5 litres

Pistachio flavouring:

1 cup currants

¼ cup rum, amaretto or other liqueur or ¼ cup fruit juice

1 cup glacé pineapple, apricots or paw paw, finely chopped

finely grated zest of 1 lemon

1 cup shelled unsalted pistachio nuts

1 cup fresh or frozen raspberries

Ice cream base:

3 eggs

10 tbsp caster sugar, divided in half

2 tbsp boiling water

2 cups cream, chilled

Line two 30 cm loaf tins or a 2.5 litre container with baking paper.

To prepare the pistachio flavouring, put the currants in a medium bowl and pour over the rum, liqueur or fruit juice. Stir, then set aside to steep for a minimum of 15 minutes or microwave for 1 minute. The alcohol helps to give the ice cream a soft texture, but the more you use the softer the ice cream will be, so don't overdo it. Stir in the pineapple, apricots or paw paw, plus the lemon zest and pistachio nuts. Reserve the berries to add later.

To make the ice cream base, separate the eggs. Place the egg whites in the largest bowl and the egg yolks in a smaller bowl, ensuring no yolk gets mixed in with the whites. Add 5 tbsp of the caster sugar to the egg whites and beat until the mixture forms stiff peaks – about 6-7 minutes. Set aside.

Add the remaining 5 tbsp of caster sugar and the boiling water to the bowl containing the three egg yolks. Beat until pale, thick and ribbony. You will know it is ready when it holds a figure of eight.

In a third bowl, beat the cream to soft peaks. Try not to overwhip it, but if you do, add a bit more cold cream and beat again. Gently fold the egg yolks and cream into the beaten egg whites using a large flat spoon. This is your Ice Cream Base.

To make Pistachio and Berry Ice Cream, add the pistachio mixture and fold together. Fold in the raspberries right at the end, reserving a few berries for a garnish. Pour the mixture into the prepared loaf tins or container.

Freeze for at least 4 hours, or preferably overnight, until set. If you're freezing the ice cream for longer, be sure to cover it to prevent freezer burn or flavour taint. To serve, lift the ice cream out of the tin or container, cut it into slices and garnish with fresh raspberries.

Watch Annabel make this recipe at thefreerangecook.com

Raspberry Ripple Ice Cream

Swirl raspberry jam through my magical Ice Cream Base (see page 227) to create an all-time favourite for kids and adults alike.

Prep time	20 mins + at least 4 hours freezing time
Makes	1¾ litres

1 recipe Ice Cream Base
(see page 227)

1 cup raspberry jam

To serve:
fresh raspberries

Prepare the Ice Cream Base as per the instructions for Pistachio and Berry Ice Cream. Instead of the pistachio mixture and raspberries, swirl 1 cup raspberry jam through the ice cream mixture.

Freeze for at least 4 hours, or preferably overnight, until set. Serve with fresh raspberries.

Double Chocolate Ice Cream

This is a decadent ice cream studded with chocolate chips that makes an extra special dessert when drizzled with my Chocolate Ganache (see page 240).

Prep time	20 mins + at least 4 hours freezing time
Makes	2½ litres

1 recipe Ice Cream Base
(see page 227)

1 cup Chocolate Ganache
(see page 240)

1 cup chocolate chips

To serve:
chocolate shavings
or Chocolate Ganache
(see page 240)

Prepare the Ice Cream Base as per the instructions for Pistachio and Berry Ice Cream. Instead of the pistachio mixture and raspberries, swirl 1 cup Chocolate Ganache and 1 cup chocolate chips through the ice cream mixture. Freeze for at least 4 hours, or preferably overnight, until set.

Serve sprinkled with chocolate shavings or drizzled with Chocolate Ganache.

Happy hens

When our children were little, our family were the lucky recipients of four baby chickens from the local kindergarten.

Each year, the kindy would hatch a clutch of eggs in an incubator. For an egg to hatch, it needs to sit point-down at exactly 37.5°C for 21 days. For 18 days, it needs to be gently rocked several times a day, then for the last three days it needs to be left to settle. After three weeks, little balls of chirping golden fluff emerge, a miracle of nature that never ceases to please.

Fluffy, Browny, Whitey and Woody came to live in our garden and for several years they provided a bountiful supply of eggs. I loved the way they recycled the scraps, their poo would fire up the compost bin, and, as long as they didn't get into the vege garden, they were free range weed eaters. But the best part was going out each morning to get the eggs – as soon as you hear that particular rising cackle you know a hen has laid. A regular supply of leafy greens and weeds ensured orange yolks, and I swear they were the best-tasting eggs of all time.

As a rule, chicken breeds with white earlobes lay white eggs and those with red lobes lay brown eggs. There is no difference in flavour or nutrition. To find out how old eggs are, drop them into a bowl of cold water – fresh eggs will lie on their side, but as they age they absorb more air and turn upright, finally floating when they are rotten.

From when a chicken starts laying at 20 weeks until it is a year old, it is called a pullet. Pullet eggs are smaller than eggs laid by adult chickens – I'd use two in a recipe calling for one normal egg.

A recent visit to heritage poultry breeder John Davies in Waimate rekindled my enthusiasm for chickens, and I brought home two Barnevelder pullets to start my brood (the heavier breeds are usually more docile). Next I'm eyeing up a couple of John's black and white stippled Plymouth Barred Rocks. But that's another trip to look forward to.

Strawberry Lemon Puff

A lot of people feel nervous about the idea of making choux pastry, but it's remarkably easy once you know how. And mastering it is worth the effort – this choux pastry puff will knock the socks off your friends.

Prep time	15 mins
Cook time	65 mins
Serves	6-8

Choux pastry:
½ cup water

4 tbsp (60g) butter, diced

¾ cup plain flour, sifted

1 tbsp sugar

½ tsp vanilla extract

2 large eggs

To garnish:
½ cup sliced almonds

To fill:
2 cups cream, chilled

1 cup Lemon Curd
(see page 254)

24 strawberries, sliced

To dust:
icing sugar

Preheat oven to 200°C (it is important to use the fanbake function). Mark a 22cm circle on a piece of baking paper and then draw a 18cm circle inside it to create a donut shape. An easy way to do this is to draw around two plates. Place the paper upside down on a baking tray (this stops the marks from transferring to your food).

To make the choux pastry, place the water and butter in a medium pot and heat to a rolling boil. Once the butter is fully melted, add the flour all at once and beat over the heat with a wooden spoon until the mixture leaves the sides of the saucepan and starts to crust a little on the base of the pan – about 1 minute.

Remove from the heat and transfer the batter to a cake mixer or large mixing bowl. Add sugar and vanilla and beat for 20 seconds before beating in eggs one at a time. The mixture should be thick enough to drop from a spoon in clumps, rather than falling freely.

Spread the batter between the lines on your baking paper, spreading to form a ring. Run a fork over the mixture (the puff will split while cooking and this encourages it to split along the top rather than at the sides), then sprinkle with sliced almonds. Bake at 200°C for 12 minutes then reduce the heat to 180°C and cook for a further 15-20 minutes until the puff is golden and feels firm when tapped. Turn off the oven, but leave the puff inside for another 15 minutes.

Remove the puff from the oven and transfer to a rack. When it has cooled a little, split horizontally using a serrated knife.

Assemble the puff about 30 minutes before serving. Whip the cream until it forms soft peaks then loosely fold in the Lemon Curd. Spread the lemon cream mixture over the base of the cooled ring and scatter with sliced strawberries. Replace the lid and dust liberally with sifted icing sugar. Serve in wedges.

Coffee Cream Éclairs

With my fail-safe Choux Pastry (see page 233) you're on your way to making these finger-licking dessert treats. Eclairs and profiteroles are guaranteed to impress.

Prep time	15 mins
Cook time	30 mins
Makes	8

1 recipe Choux Pastry
(see page 233)

To fill:
1¼ cups cream

4 tbsp Kahlua or Tia Maria

To ice:
2 tsp instant
coffee powder

2 tbsp boiling water

2 cups icing sugar

1 tsp vanilla extract

To garnish:
½ cup shelled unsalted
pistachio nuts, chopped

Preheat oven to 200°C (use the fanbake function) and line an oven tray with baking paper. Prepare the Choux Pastry up to the point where you are ready to shape the pastry ring.

To shape the éclairs, fit a large piping bag with a 2cm nozzle and pipe the choux mixture onto the baking paper in 8 sausage shapes, each about 12cm long. If you don't have a piping bag, use a teaspoon to shape the éclairs.

Bake the éclairs for 30 minutes until puffed and golden brown. Remove from the oven, slit the side of each éclair to release the steam, then allow to cool.

To make the filling, whip the cream until it forms soft peaks then stir in the Kahlua or Tia Maria. Cut the éclair shells in half with a serrated knife and gently spoon the flavoured cream inside.

To make the icing, stir the instant coffee into the boiling water to dissolve. Sift the icing sugar into a medium bowl. Add the coffee mixture and vanilla and stir until smooth. Glide the icing onto the éclairs using a knife that has been dipped in warm water. Garnish with chopped pistachio nuts.

Ice Cream Filled Profiteroles

Preheat oven to 200°C (use the fanbake function) and line an oven tray with baking paper. Prepare 1 recipe Choux Pastry (see page 233) and scoop dessertspoons of pastry onto the lined oven tray or use teaspoons for smaller puffs. Bake for 30 minutes until puffed and golden. Remove from oven and slit side of pastry cases to release steam, then cool. When you are ready to serve the profiteroles, gently warm 1 cup Chocolate Ganache (see page 240) in a small saucepan or microwave. Cut the profiteroles in half and fill each one with a small ball of vanilla ice cream. Sandwich the lids on top and place on a serving plate. Drizzle with warm Chocolate Ganache and serve immediately. Filled iced puffs can be stored in the freezer for easy anytime treats. Makes about 16 dessert sized puffs or 24 cocktail sized puffs.

As the first nuts
of autumn start to
fall to the ground,
our squirrel instincts
come to the fore.

The Ultimate Chocolate Cake

This is the cake that will make you a star. It will become your secret weapon for dinner parties and special occasions and you'll never look at another chocolate cake recipe again. It's so incredibly simple – a magical conjuring up that results in a huge, rich, moist cake. The same recipe even makes wonderful little Chocolate Cupcakes (see below).

Prep time	5 mins
Cook time	1 hour
Serves	12-16
Makes	1 big cake or 2 smaller cakes

3 cups self-raising flour

2 cups sugar

1½ tsp vanilla extract

¾ cup cocoa powder

2 tsp baking soda, sifted

200g butter, softened

1 cup milk or unsweetened yoghurt

3 large eggs

1 cup boiling hot coffee

To ice:
1 recipe Chocolate Ganache (see page 240)

fresh raspberries

Heat oven to 160°C. Grease the sides and line the base of a 30cm round cake tin or 2 x 20cm round cake tins with baking paper.

Place all ingredients except Chocolate Ganache and raspberries in a bowl or food processor and mix or blitz until the ingredients are combined and the butter is fully incorporated.

Pour mixture into prepared tin or tins and smooth top. Bake for 1 hour or until a skewer inserted into the centre comes out clean. Allow to cool in the tin. If not using at once, the cake will keep for about a week in a sealed container in the fridge. You can also freeze it uniced.

When you are ready to ice the cake, slather chilled Chocolate Ganache over the top. Top with fresh raspberries and serve.

Chocolate Cupcakes

Preheat oven to 160°C and line 24 muffin pans with paper cases. Prepare cake batter according to the instructions for The Ultimate Chocolate Cake (see above). Spoon mixture into the paper cases, filling about two thirds full. Bake for 25-30 minutes. Cool before icing. For icing, beat 200g firm cream cheese with 100g softened butter until smooth. Gradually beat in 2 cups icing sugar until smooth and creamy. Add a few drops of food colouring to get the desired colour. Icing can be stored in the fridge in a sealed container for up to a week. Pipe onto the cakes and top with confectionery sprinkles. Makes 24.

Chocolate Ganache

It's hard to believe this luxurious chocolate sauce contains only two ingredients –
equal quantities of cream and the best quality chocolate you can lay your hands on.
I like to use chocolate containing at least 70 per cent cocoa solids. Chocolate Ganache
is a handy Fridge Fixing that can be used as an indulgent icing for cakes (see page 238)
or profiteroles (see page 235) or stirred into ice cream (see page 229). It also makes
a divine dip for strawberries. To make Spiked Chocolate Sauce, stir 2 tbsp Kahlua
(for a coffee flavour) or Cointreau (for an orange flavour) into the finished ganache.

Prep time	5 mins
Cook time	5 mins
	+ standing
Makes	approx 4 cups

500ml cream

500g best quality dark
chocolate, roughly chopped

Pour the cream into a medium pot and heat it until it is almost but
not quite boiling. You'll know it's ready when bubbles start to form
around the edge of the pot. Remove from the heat and add the
chocolate. Stand for 2 minutes, then stir until the chocolate is fully
melted into the cream. Whisk until smooth and glossy. When you
start to stir it, you think it won't come together, but it will.

If you're not using the ganache straight away, store it in a jar in the
fridge for up to two weeks. When you're ready to serve it, gently
warm in a pot or microwave to soften.

Chocolate Truffles

Mix 1 cup warmed Chocolate Ganache (see above) with 3 tbsp softened butter until evenly incorporated.
Stir in 4 tsp Cointreau or other liqueur. Chill mixture for 1 hour or until it is firm enough to mould. When
mixture is firm, sieve ½ cup good quality cocoa into a bowl. Use two teaspoons to scoop out balls of
chocolate mixture. Roll each ball between your hands to get an even shape and then roll in cocoa to coat.
If the mixture softens as you go, return to the fridge until it sets enough to be workable. Makes about 15.

The sensory experience of food isn't just about the taste. The luxe of chocolate lies also in its exquisite aroma and silky, smooth texture.

Chocolate and Cranberry Slice

This luscious melt-and-stir chocolate slice is a decadent treat to finish a meal.
As a variation, use hazelnuts and dried apricots instead of cranberries and pistachios.

Prep time	15 mins
Cook time	2 mins
	+ 1 hour chilling
Makes	approx 30 slices

350g best quality dark chocolate, chopped

¾ cup sweetened condensed milk

2 tsp vanilla extract

¼ cup icing sugar

1 cup dried cranberries

¾ cup shelled unsalted pistachio nuts

Line a small 16 x 5cm loaf tin with baking paper.

Melt the chocolate over a double boiler or in a microwave (microwave for 1-2 minutes, stirring every 30 seconds). Take it off the heat when nearly melted. If overheated it can 'clump up' and go hard. The residual heat will be enough to fully melt it.

Add the sweetened condensed milk and stir until evenly combined, then stir in the vanilla, icing sugar, cranberries and pistachio nuts. At this point the mixture will solidify.

Press the mixture firmly into the prepared loaf tin. Chill until set, then slice and store in a cool place. This rich chocolate slice keeps for several weeks in an airtight container.

Espresso Hazelnut Ripple

This is a wonderfully indulgent after dinner treat adapted from a recipe given to me by clever cook and caterer Annie Bastow. It not only tastes great, but it looks dramatic too with a mix of dark and white chocolate swirled across the top.

Prep time	15 mins + chilling
Cook time	15 mins (to roast the nuts)
Serves	10-12

1½ cups shelled hazelnuts or other nuts

375g white chocolate

375g best quality dark chocolate

2 tsp finely ground espresso coffee beans

Line a shallow baking tray or roasting dish measuring at least 35 x 25cm with baking paper.

Roast the hazelnuts at 180°C for 12-15 minutes until they smell aromatic. Allow to cool and then rub off the loose skins in a clean teatowel. (Don't worry about doing a perfect job – they don't need to be fully skinned).

Place the white chocolate in a double boiler or microwave and melt (if using a microwave, heat for about 2 minutes, stirring after 1 minute and then every 30 seconds until chocolate is melted and smooth).

Melt the dark chocolate in a separate bowl, using the same method. It tends to take a little longer.

Mix most of the hazelnuts into the melted white chocolate. Roughly mark 5 long rows onto the lined tray. Spread the white chocolate mix into the 2nd and 4th rows. Sprinkle extra nuts where needed.

Mix the ground coffee into the dark chocolate. Spread this mixture into the other 3 rows. Pull a knife across the rows 3 or 4 times each way to create swirls.

Chill until set and then cut or break into chunks. Serve on a platter with coffee or accompany with fresh berries.

Tropical Marshmallows

This recipe calls for an electric mixer and a candy thermometer, but it is remarkably easy and delivers a real wow factor.

Prep time	15 mins
Cook time	25 mins
	+ 3 hours
	standing time
Makes	28 pieces

grapeseed or other neutral oil, for greasing

1½ cups coarse thread coconut

½ cup icing sugar

2 tbsp cornflour

½ cup orange juice (2 large oranges)

¼ cup fresh lime juice (2 large limes)

6 tsp powdered gelatine

2 cups caster sugar

1 cup water

2 egg whites, at room temperature

pinch of salt

Lightly grease a shallow dish measuring approx 35 x 20cm with neutral oil. Combine thread coconut, icing sugar and cornflour and spread half of the mixture evenly across the base of the prepared dish. Reserve the rest to dust the top of the marshmallow.

Place the orange and lime juice in a small bowl, sprinkle gelatine over the top and set aside. Place caster sugar and water in a saucepan and cook over a low heat, stirring, until the sugar dissolves. Increase the heat to medium and boil until the syrup reaches 125°C on a sugar thermometer – about 15 minutes.

While the syrup is boiling, place the egg whites and salt in a clean, grease-free bowl and whisk with an electric mixer until frothy.

As soon as the sugar syrup reaches 125°C, remove it from the heat, add gelatine mixture and stir until gelatine dissolves (it bubbles up a bit when first added). Gradually add the hot citrus gelatine syrup to the whisked egg whites, whisking continuously on medium speed until the mixture has doubled in size. Keep beating at a lower speed until the bowl feels just warm to the touch – about 8-10 minutes. Pour into prepared dish and spread evenly with a lightly oiled spatula.

Dust the top liberally with the other half of the coconut mixture. Stand at room temperature until firm – about 3 hours. Using a sharp, hot, dry knife, cut the marshmallow into 6 or 7 strips widthwise, and then slice lengthwise into 4. Roll in any loose coconut sugar to coat.

If you're not using the marshmallows at once, transfer to a storage container, sprinkling with leftover coconut sugar and separating the layers with sheets of waxed paper. They will keep in an airtight container at room temperature for 2-3 weeks. These marshmallows are divine toasted – skewer them with wooden chopsticks and grill over the embers of a fire, or use a blow torch to caramelise them.

In simple rituals like
toasting marshmallows
we create food memories
that last a lifetime.

Caramelised Onion and Feta Tart

∾

Braised Oxtails with Star Anise
Parsnip and Carrot Mash
Gingered Bok Choy

∾

Ruby Roasted Pears
with Crème Fraîche

from the orchard

The fruition of a season's growth is captured in juicy, fragrant sweetness, mouthwatering desserts and baking.

BIG ORGANIC
PLUMS
PICK YOUR OWN
$2·25   Kg.

To the uninitiated, the sensory experience of a piece of fruit, picked at the perfect point of ripeness and devoured sun-warmed from the tree, offers an epiphany of sorts. Its juice will stain your shirt and you will not, for that particular moment, care, lost in an explosion of taste and juiciness, marvelling that something so simple could create such pleasure.

When the children were young, we spent a summer in Sicily, shopping each week down the coast at the market in Trapani. By sheer fluke we arrived one day to the most exquisite aroma of peach. I zigzagged my way around the whole market before locating an old man with his little box of the world's most fragrant white peaches – the entire crop picked that morning from the tree in his yard. I bought the lot, just 13 heavenly, exquisitely aromatic, soft-skinned, juiciest-ever white peaches. In pure unadulterated greed I devoured them all in a single afternoon – with no regrets.

Ever since, I have tried to find that particular white peach, or something akin to it, for my own orchard but nothing has come close to matching the meltingly aromatic sweet juiciness. And maybe that is good, as the experience is etched into my memory and with it other snapshots from that particular day – my six-year-old daughter Rose, in long plaits and stripy pink dress, laughing in delight over her giant gelato, a fisherman and his son in their little blue and white boat fixing their net, the way the light fell onto a wall of scarlet bougainvillea. So our memories are built, ephemeral moments of pleasure fleshed out, tucked away in our minds to bring out and savour again at some later, perhaps less inspiring or energetic, time. And all thanks to a peach.

Lemon Curd

You'll need a double boiler to make this versatile Fridge Fixing. If you don't have one, improvise with two pots, one slightly bigger than the other, or a pot and a heatproof glass or metal bowl. Partially fill the bigger pot with water and bring to a simmer, then sit the smaller pot or the bowl over the top. The indirect heat is perfect for cooking delicate ingredients like eggs. Lemon Curd is lovely stirred into a parfait (see below) or spooned into tiny pastry cases (see page 257).

Prep time	10 mins
Cook time	12-15 mins
Makes	approx 4 cups

1½ cups caster sugar

220g butter, diced

finely grated zest of 1 lemon

1¼ cups lemon juice (about 6 juicy lemons), strained

6 large eggs

Thoroughly wash and sterilise 4 medium jars and their pop-top lids. Place the sugar, butter, lemon zest and juice in a heatproof bowl over a pot of boiling water, making sure the water does not touch the bottom of the bowl, or in a double boiler. Heat over a medium heat until the butter has melted.

Whisk the eggs in a separate bowl and stir them into the butter mixture. Cook over a gentle heat, stirring constantly with a wooden spoon, until the mixture thickens enough to coat the back of the spoon – about 3-5 minutes. Make sure the mixture doesn't boil. It's ready when the lemon curd holds a line when you run your finger across the back of the coated spoon.

Remove from the heat immediately, stirring a little to stop it from overheating on the base. Don't worry if it seems a little runny: it will thicken as it cools. Pour the hot mixture through a strainer into a jug to remove any lemon zest or flecks of egg white, then pour it into the hot sterilised jars and seal. Lemon curd will keep for several weeks in the fridge.

Lemon Curd Parfait

Place 600ml cream and 1 tsp vanilla in a large bowl and whip until the cream forms soft peaks. Loosely fold through ¾ cup Lemon Curd (see above) and 4 roughly crushed meringues. Spoon into parfait glasses, cover and chill for up to 6 hours. Serve garnished with diced kiwifruit or other fruit and a sprinkle of toasted thread coconut. Parfaits will keep in the fridge for up to 6 hours. Serves 4-6.

Lemon Curd Tarts

These tiny tarts are an indulgent accompaniment to coffee or great as part of a dessert platter. They're made using my Lemon Curd (see page 254) and my fail-safe polenta pastry. This pastry is perfect if you're short of time because it doesn't need to be baked blind. You could also spoon the curd into any kind of pre-cooked sweet pastry cases.

Prep time	10 mins
	+ resting
Cook time	20-25 mins
Makes	30 mini tarts

Polenta pastry:

150g butter, softened

⅔ cup sugar

1 egg

1⅔ cups flour

½ cup polenta

To fill:

1½ cups Lemon Curd
(see page 254)

To garnish:

30 fresh raspberries

Preheat oven to 160°C and grease 30 mini muffin pans. Put the softened butter and the sugar in a medium mixing bowl and cream together until light and fluffy. Mix in the egg and then add the flour and the polenta, a little at a time, until evenly combined.

Put the pastry aside to rest for 20 minutes, then roll it out on a lightly floured board to a thickness of 5mm. Use a cookie cutter to cut 30 small circles (approx 5cm) from the pastry, then use them to line your muffin pans, pressing out to cover the base and sides. Bake for 20-25 minutes until crispy and golden. Cool completely.

If you don't plan to use the cases that day, store them in an airtight container. Up to two hours before serving, fill them with Lemon Curd and garnish with a fresh raspberry in the centre of each.

Berry Syrup

This useful Fridge Fixing can be used as a tangy sauce for desserts, swirled through yoghurt or whipped cream, or drizzled over The Ultimate Chocolate Cake (see page 238). If you're short on time, simply scoop ice cream into pretty bowls or glasses, pour on Berry Syrup and garnish with fresh berries.

Prep time	5 mins
Cook time	2 mins
Makes	1¾ cups

3 cups raspberries, fresh or thawed from frozen

½ cup caster sugar

2 tbsp water

Put the berries in a pot and add the sugar and water. Bring to a simmer. Remove the pot from the heat and press the berries through a sieve or mouli to extract the juice and remove the pips. Berry Syrup will keep for up to 10 days covered in the fridge.

Berry Syrup and Yoghurt Parfait

Take 2 punnets of fresh raspberries and drop a few raspberries into the bottom of 6-8 stemmed glasses. Top with yoghurt and drizzle with Berry Syrup (see above). Finish with more raspberries. Serves 6-8.

Those fleeting harvests
that last for just a few
weeks each year give us
something to look forward
to and briefly savour.

Strawberry Cloud Cake

This stunning dessert is a piece of magic. It looks really impressive with very little effort and you can get it ready early in the day or a few days ahead so you're free to relax when your friends arrive. You can use any kind of berries for the topping. The coconut lends a tropical taste and interesting texture to the base.

Prep time	15 mins
Freeze time	4 hours
Serves	10-12

150g plain sweet biscuits

½ cup desiccated coconut

1½ tsp ground cinnamon

100g butter, melted

To fill:
2 egg whites, at room temperature

1 cup sugar

250g (1 punnet) ripe strawberries, hulled and sliced

1 tbsp lemon juice

1 tsp vanilla extract

To garnish:
fresh raspberries

Berry Syrup
(see page 258)

Line the base of a 26-28cm spring form cake tin with baking paper or waxed paper. This makes it easy to lift the cake out later.

Make the base by putting the biscuits in a brown paper bag and crushing them into crumbs by beating carefully with a rolling pin. Pour the crumbs into a medium bowl and add the coconut, cinnamon and melted butter. Stir well to combine.

Press firmly into the base of the prepared tin. It doesn't need to be a thick layer – just enough to cover the bottom of the tin. Refrigerate the base while you prepare the filling.

Place egg whites, sugar, sliced strawberries, lemon juice and vanilla in the clean, dry bowl of an electric mixer. Beat on high speed for about 6-8 minutes until the mixture is very thick and fluffy and the sugar has dissolved. To test whether it is ready, rub a bit of the mixture between your fingers. You should not feel any gritty sugar. If you do, beat a little longer.

Spoon the filling over the chilled base, smooth the top, cover with a sheet of baking paper and freeze for at least 4 hours. The cake will keep in an airtight container in the freezer for up to a month.

To serve, cut cake into wedges using a knife that has been warmed in hot water. Garnish with fresh raspberries on top and drizzle with Berry Syrup to serve.

Raspberry Chocolate Tarts

Unctuous, creamy chocolate meets tart raspberries and crunchy, buttery sweet pastry in these divine little mouthfuls of bliss.

Prep time	15 mins +
	10 mins chilling
Cook time	22-25 mins
Makes	30 mini tarts

Sweet pastry:
360g butter, softened

¾ cup sugar

1 egg

3⅓ cups flour

pinch of salt

To fill:
1 recipe Chocolate Ganache
(see page 240)

To garnish:
30 fresh raspberries

To make the sweet pastry, place the butter and sugar in a bowl and beat together until fluffy and creamy. Add the egg and beat to combine. Add the flour and the salt and mix until just combined. Lightly flour your hands, then pat the dough (it will be quite soft) into 3 or more portions. If you're not using the pastry immediately, seal it in waxed paper and chill or freeze until required.

When you are ready to make the tarts, grease 30 mini muffin pans (approx 5cm in diameter). Roll out the pastry between two sheets of baking paper until it is about 5mm thick. Cut out pastry rounds to fit your muffin pans, then press into the tins and repair any cracks. Chill for at least 10 minutes while you preheat oven to 160°C.

Bake blind for 12-15 minutes, or until you can lift out the baking paper and baking beans or rice without it sticking to the pastry. Be careful not to overcook the pastry or it will be too dark when cooked for the second time.

Return empty cases to the oven until pastry is golden and crisp – another 10 minutes. Allow pastry cases to cool before removing from tins.

Pipe chilled Chocolate Ganache into the cooled pastry cases. If you prefer a smooth finish, warm the Chocolate Ganache and pour it into the tart cases. Chill until the filling is set – about an hour. Just before serving, garnish each tart with a fresh raspberry.

Chocolate Cherry Tiramisu

Some recipes make this classic dessert unnecessarily complicated, but this version is dead easy and wickedly good. Traditionally, tiramisu contains coffee or alcohol, but I've made this with Berry Syrup (see page 258) so the kids can enjoy it too. If you're short on time, use store-bought chocolate cake or sponge.

Prep time	15 mins + 4-24 hours chilling
Serves	8-10

4 eggs, separated

2 cups (400g) mascarpone

4 tbsp brown sugar

1 tsp vanilla extract

23cm chocolate cake or chocolate sponge (approx 300g), broken into 2cm cubes

1 cup Berry Syrup (see page 258)

800g fresh cherries, pitted, or 500g fresh or frozen raspberries or other berries

To garnish:
1¼ cups cream

2 tbsp cocoa

Combine the egg yolks, mascarpone, sugar and vanilla extract in a bowl and using a wooden spoon beat until thick and creamy. Put to one side.

Put the egg whites in a clean bowl and beat with a clean whisk until they form soft peaks. Fold gently into the mascarpone mixture.

Place one third of the sponge pieces in the base of a large glass serving bowl. Drizzle a third of the Berry Syrup over the top. Spoon over half the mascarpone mixture then cover with half the pitted cherries or berries.

Layer on another third of the sponge pieces, drizzle with another third of the syrup and top with the remainder of the mascarpone. Top with the rest of the cherries or berries, another layer of sponge and the last of the syrup. Cover and chill for at least 4 hours or up to 24 hours.

Just before serving, whip the cream until it forms soft peaks and spread it over the top of the tiramisu. Sieve the cocoa over the top and chill until ready to serve.

Prawn and Mint Finger Rolls
with Chilli Lime Dipping Sauce

∽

Spicy Chicken Skewers
with Chermoula Dipping Sauce
Creamy Moroccan Cucumber Salad
Corn and Avocado Salad
Potato Salad with Capers and Mint

∽

Chocolate Cherry Tiramisu
Tropical Marshmallows

Individual Rhubarb and Berry Crumbles

The trick to not having a soggy crumble is to thicken the fruit juices by mixing a little cornflour into the raw fruit before cooking. I like to make Crumble Topping in bulk as it can be frozen or stored in the fridge for up to four weeks. This recipe makes more than you'll need for one crumble, so use the extra with fresh berries and yoghurt or in a caramel slice (see page 271) or as a crunchy cake topping (see page 272).

Prep time	5 mins
Cook time	35-40 mins
Serves	6-8

Crumble topping:

2 cups flour

1 cup ground almonds
(or use a total of 3 cups flour)

1½ cups brown sugar,
packed tightly

2 cups rolled oats,
finest cut available

1 cup almonds,
chopped or slivered

2 tsp mixed spice

250g butter, melted

Fruit filling:

500g fresh rhubarb, peeled and chopped into 1cm pieces

400g berries

2 tsp cornflour

½ cup sugar

To serve:
Crème Fraîche
(see page 224),
vanilla ice cream
or whipped cream

a few fresh raspberries

Preheat oven to 160°C. First prepare the crumble topping by placing all the dry ingredients in a large mixing bowl and stirring well to combine. Add the melted butter and mix with a wooden spoon until evenly combined.

Divide rhubarb and berries between six to eight 15cm ramekins. Mix the cornflour with the sugar and sprinkle it evenly over the fruit.

Spread about ½ cup of Crumble Topping evenly over the fruit in each ramekin, pressing down firmly. Bake until golden and crisp – about 40 minutes. Serve topped with a spoon of Crème Fraîche, vanilla ice cream or whipped cream and accompanied by fresh raspberries.

Store the remaining Crumble Topping in the fridge or freezer for later use.

Fresh Berry Yoghurt Crumble

Toasted Crumble Topping (see page 268) adds sweetness and texture to natural yoghurt while the blueberries provide a fruity flavour pop on the tongue. I like to keep this toasted topping on hand in an airtight container for quick snacks and easy desserts.

Prep time	5 mins
Cook time	20-30 mins
Serves	6

2 cups Crumble Topping
(see page 268)

3 cups thick natural yoghurt
(such as Greek yoghurt)

a punnet of fresh blueberries

Preheat oven to 160°C. Spread out the Crumble Topping on a baking tray and bake, stirring occasionally, until crispy and golden – about 20-30 minutes. Allow to cool.

To assemble your yoghurt crumbles, scoop ½ cup yoghurt into each of 6 glasses or ramekins. Sprinkle each serve with 2-3 tbsp of toasted Crumble Topping and finish with a few blueberries. Any leftover toasted Crumble Topping will keep fresh for several weeks in an airtight container.

Caramel Crumble Slice

If you've got some Crumble Topping (see page 268) you're only 40 minutes away from this dangerously moreish slice.

Prep time	10 mins
Cook time	35-40 mins
Makes	approx 20 slices

3 cups Crumble Topping
(see page 268)

3 cups rolled oats

395g can sweetened
condensed milk

250g white chocolate, melted

Preheat oven to 160°C. Line a 30 x 22cm sponge roll tin with baking paper.

In a large bowl, mix together the Crumble Topping ingredients and rolled oats. Stir in the condensed milk until everything is evenly combined. Press the mixture into the prepared sponge roll tin and bake for 35-40 minutes until golden and crisp. Cut into 3 x 10cm bars whilst still hot then allow to cool in tin.

Break white chocolate into chunks and place in a dry microwave-proof bowl. Microwave for 1 minute, stirring every 20 seconds, until melted or melt in a double boiler. Drizzle melted chocolate over cooled slice. Store in an airtight container in a cool place.

Blueberry Crumble Cake

This is another wonderful way to use my Crumble Topping (see page 268). In summer I like to make this cake with stone fruit instead of berries – use 6-8 plums or apricots with their stones discarded and their flesh cut into wedges. In spring rhubarb is nice – use 3-4 stalks, finely chopped. In autumn try feijoas or apples cut into chunks, and flavour the crumble topping with 1 tsp of ginger instead of cinnamon.

Prep time	15 mins
Cook time	50-60 mins
Serves	8-10

140g butter, softened

1 cup sugar

2 eggs, at room temperature

1 tsp vanilla extract

¾ cup plain yoghurt

2 cups flour

3 tsp baking powder

½ tsp baking soda

2 cups fresh or frozen blueberries

1½ cups Crumble Topping (see page 268)

Preheat oven to 180°C. Grease the sides of a 25cm spring-form or loose-bottomed cake tin and line the base with baking paper.

Beat the butter and sugar together until they are pale and fluffy. Add the eggs and vanilla and beat well. Beat in the yoghurt, then add the sifted flour, baking powder and baking soda and stir gently until just combined. (The mixture will be a very thick consistency). Spread into the prepared tin, sprinkle with the blueberries and then sprinkle the Crumble Topping over the top.

Bake for about 50-60 minutes until the cake is golden and a wooden skewer inserted into the middle comes out clean. Stand for 15 minutes before turning out of the tin, then allow to cool before cutting. Store in an airtight container.

In this busy world,
cooking is the ultimate
form of living in the now.

Sticky Date Pudding

This is my twist on an old favourite. It's also one of those brilliant recipes where you don't have to cream the butter and sugar. To create individual desserts or a lunchbox treat, cut up the pears into smaller slices or chunks and cook the mixture in muffin pans.

Prep time	10 mins
Cook time	35-40 mins
Serves	8

1 cup pitted dates

1¼ cups water

1 tsp baking soda

60g butter, chopped

1 packed cup brown sugar

2 eggs

1½ cups self-raising flour

1 tsp vanilla extract

1 tsp ground ginger

2 pears, cored and cut into thin slices

To serve:
Wicked Toffee Sauce
(see below)

Preheat oven to 180°C. Grease the sides of a 25cm cake tin and line the base with baking paper.

Place dates, water and baking soda in a pot large enough to hold the entire mixture and boil for 5 minutes. Remove from the heat and mash with a potato masher to break up the dates.

Stir in chopped butter and mix until butter is melted. Mix in sugar and eggs then fold in flour, vanilla and ginger.

Arrange pear slices in a concentric circle around the base of the tin, placing a few slices in the centre. Pour batter over the top and smooth evenly to fully cover the pears.

Bake for 35-40 minutes until golden and a skewer inserted in the centre comes out clean. Stand for at least 10 minutes before turning upside down onto a serving platter and removing the baking paper. Serve with warm Wicked Toffee Sauce.

This dessert keeps well for a day or two and can be frozen. Thaw and serve warm – heat it in the oven for 10 minutes or microwave it for 2-3 minutes.

Wicked Toffee Sauce

Place ½ cup water in a saucepan. Add 2 cups caster sugar and place over a medium heat until the sugar dissolves and comes to the boil, swirling the pot now and then. Boil without stirring until mixture turns a golden caramel colour – approximately 8-10 minutes. (Do not be tempted to stir the mixture as this could cause it to crystallise. To prevent it from crystallising, you can run a wet brush around the sides of the pot, allowing the excess water to run into the sugar mixture.) Remove from heat, add 2 cups cream and 2 tsp vanilla extract and stir until smooth. Leftover sauce can be stored in the fridge and reheated. Makes 3 cups.

Vanilla Plum Cake

This great recipe makes either one huge cake or two medium dessert cakes – one to eat straight away and one for the freezer. Vary the fruit according to what's in season – you can use plums, apricots or peaches.

Prep time	20 mins
Cook time	50-60 mins
Serves	10-12

12 plums or apricots,
or 6 peaches

300g butter

1½ cups sugar

3 eggs

finely grated zest of 1 lemon

1 tsp vanilla extract

1 cup buttermilk or yoghurt

3½ cups self raising flour

To dust:
2 tbsp icing sugar

Preheat oven to 160°C. Grease one roasting dish or two 20cm springform cake tins and line with baking paper. Halve the plums or apricots or quarter the peaches and put to one side.

Cream together the butter and sugar. Beat in the eggs one at a time. Mix in the lemon zest and vanilla. Gently stir in the buttermilk or yoghurt and the flour until evenly combined. Do not overmix.

Spoon the batter into the prepared roasting dish or cake tins. Spread it out evenly, smoothing the top, then arrange the fruit on top, cut side up.

Bake for 50-60 minutes until the cake is set and golden. The fruit will sink into the cake as it cooks. If you're not planning to eat the cake that day it can be frozen for later use. Dust with icing sugar to serve.

Plum Muffins

Preheat oven to 160°C and lightly grease 30 muffin pans. Halve 15 plums and discard the stones. Follow the recipe for Vanilla Plum Cake (see above) and spoon the mixture into the muffin pans, allowing 1 rounded tablespoon per muffin. Arrange half a plum, cut side up, on top of each muffin. Bake for 25 minutes until set and golden. Remove from the oven and leave the muffins to cool for at least 15 minutes before removing them from the pans. Dust with icing sugar to serve. Makes 30.

In the simple act of baking, pleasure given is pleasure gained.

Grilled Summer Fruit and Figs

Grilled fresh fruit makes a really speedy and easy dessert. Here I've halved peaches, apricots and figs, but you can use whichever summer fruits you can get your hands on. A drizzle of warm Port Wine Syrup (see below) adds the finishing touch.

Prep time	10 mins
Cook time	8-10 mins
Serves	6

1kg mixed peaches, apricots and/or figs, washed

½ cup icing sugar

To serve:
½ recipe Port Wine Syrup
(see below)

Halve the fruit and remove the stones from the peaches and apricots. Place the fruit cut side up in a roasting dish and sift the icing sugar evenly over the top.

Place under a hot grill about 10cm from the heat source. Grill until the sugar is bubbling and starting to caramelise – 8-10 minutes. Drizzle with warm Port Wine Syrup and serve immediately.

Port Wine Syrup

This rich syrup is wonderful drizzled over fresh or cooked fruit desserts like Grilled Summer Fruit and Figs (see above). I like to make it in bulk and keep it in the fridge – it lasts for weeks and reheats well.

Prep time	5 mins
Cook time	10 mins
Makes	1½ cups

1 cup red wine

1 cup port

1 cup honey

1 cinnamon quill

Place the wine, port, honey and cinnamon quill in a frypan or wide-bottomed saucepan. Bring to the boil, stirring occasionally. Boil hard until the liquid has reduced by half – about 10 minutes. Remove the cinnamon quill and serve the sauce warm, drizzled over grilled fruit.

Ruby Roasted Pears

These pears are first poached and then roasted, which gives them a wonderfully intense flavour and deep burnished hue. They taste best if poached and chilled in their liquid for up to three days before roasting, so they can absorb the flavours and colour of the syrup.

Prep time	15 mins + chilling time
Cook time	50 mins to poach + 12-15 mins to roast
Serves	6-8

2 cups sugar

3 cups red wine
(or use pomegranate juice)

2 cinnamon sticks

4 bay leaves

1 vanilla pod

6-8 just-ripe pears,
with stems intact

To serve:
Crème Fraîche
(see page 224)

Choose a pot that will fit 6-8 pears sitting snugly upright in a single layer. Heat sugar, wine, cinnamon sticks, bay leaves and vanilla pod, stirring until the sugar has dissolved.

Peel pears, leaving them whole with stalks intact. Slice or peel the base of each pear so it will stand upright. Place in the pot with the poaching liquid, arranging the pears so they are covered as much as possible by the syrup. Simmer gently for 30 minutes or until tender, turning occasionally.

Cool pears then place with their syrup in a container, cover and chill for at least 24 hours or up to 3 days, turning occasionally so that they colour evenly.

Lift pears out of the syrup and arrange in a shallow baking dish. Place the syrup in a pot, bring to a rapid boil and continue cooking until reduced by half – about 20 minutes. Remove bay leaves, cinnamon and vanilla pod. You can rinse and dry the vanilla pod and then store it in a sugar container to use again.

When you are ready to serve the pears, preheat oven to 220°C. Baste the pears liberally with syrup, ensuring they are well coated, and roast for 12-15 minutes. Brush with more syrup as they come out of the oven. Place on serving plates, drizzle with a large spoonful of syrup and accompany with Crème Fraîche.

Baked Apples with Crème Anglaise

Tart baking apples become sublimely soft and rich when stuffed with an intensely flavoured mix of dates, walnuts and spices and slow-baked in the oven to caramelise.

Prep time	30 mins
Cook time	approx 1 hour (depending on size of apples)
Serves	6

6 tart or baking apples such as Granny Smith or Braeburn

20 pitted dates, chopped

⅓ cup chopped walnuts

6 tbsp brown sugar

2 tsp ground cinnamon

1 tsp ground cloves

½ cup water

2 tbsp maple syrup

6 tsp butter

To serve:
Crème Anglaise
(see page 224)

Preheat oven to 160°C. Remove cores from the apples in a neat plug. Use a paring knife to enlarge the cavity to 2.5cm in diameter. Score the skin around the circumference of each apple with a sharp knife (this allows them to split neatly around the middle when they cook).

Combine dates, walnuts, sugar, cinnamon and cloves. Stuff the mixture into the apples and place them in a shallow baking dish.

Drizzle the water and maple syrup over the apples. Dot each apple with 1 teaspoon butter and bake them until they are wrinkly and soft and starting to puff. This should take about 1 hour, depending on the size of the apples.

Serve hot accompanied by a dish of Crème Anglaise.

VINEYARD
OPERATIONAL
AREA

Verjuice

What I love about this recipe is that it uses unripened grapes that might otherwise have gone to waste. You can buy commercially-produced Verjuice, but with very little effort you can create your own. One of the benefits of Verjuice is that it gives an amazing flavour without adding fat. If you don't use it all straight away you can freeze any leftovers – the freshly picked unripe grapes freeze well too.

Prep time	10 mins
Makes	3 cups

1.6kg unripe grapes

Purée the grapes in a food processor. Press the pulp through a strainer lined with 4-5 layers of fine muslin to remove the skins and seeds. Pour the juice into a jug or bottle and refrigerate for use within 12 hours or freeze for later use.

Pears in Verjuice

This dessert looks and tastes so classy on the plate, but it's a dream to make. Choose a saucepan that will snugly fit 6 pears sitting upright in a single layer. As the pears poach they absorb the tart flavour of the Verjuice (see above) and this is perfectly offset by the sweetness of the honey and the spiciness of the cinnamon.

Prep time	15 mins
Cook time	30 mins
Serves	6

6 just-ripe pears
with stems intact

3 cups (750ml) Verjuice
(see above)

¼ cup honey

1 cinnamon quill

Peel the pears, leaving them whole with their stalks intact. Take a fine slice off the bottom of each pear to enable them to stand for serving. Put to one side.

Place Verjuice, honey and cinnamon quill into a pot and bring to a simmer, stirring once or twice. Add the pears and poach for 30 minutes, turning occasionally.

Remove the pears from the pot and reduce the sauce by two thirds. Serve the pears drizzled with sauce. They will keep for over a week in the fridge.

Verjuice Nectarine Jelly

Homemade jelly is a lovely light dessert that you can make up to a day ahead. I love the flavour the Verjuice (see page 287) gives, but you can also make this jelly using any fruit juice or even a riesling wine. Use your imagination by flavouring it with any fruit of your choice.

Prep time	15 mins
	+ 3 hours
	setting time
Cook time	5 mins
Serves	6-8

3 cups (750ml) Verjuice
(see page 287)
or riesling wine

1 cup sugar

1 vanilla pod, split lengthways
or 1 tsp vanilla paste or extract

5 tsp gelatine

½ cup water

3 nectarines, cut into fine dice,
and 100g green grapes, halved,
or about 400g of any fresh fruit
(except kiwifruit or papaya as
the jellies won't set)

Put the Verjuice, sugar and vanilla pod in a pot and heat until nearly boiling. Turn off the heat and leave to steep for 10 minutes.

Lift out the vanilla pod without scraping out the seeds. Rinse and dry it and store it in your sugar jar to use again later.

Sprinkle the gelatine over the water, stirring until it is evenly absorbed. Mix the soaked gelatine into the hot Verjuice liquid and stir until it is fully dissolved. You will know it is ready when there are no gelatine granules left on the spoon.

Divide the fruit between 6-8 glasses or bowls and pour the Verjuice liquid over the top. Allow to set in the fridge for at least 3 hours. Remove the set jellies from the fridge 10 minutes before serving.

Sweet honey bees

It's hard not to like honey. The sweet nectar of flowers, collected and concentrated by clever little honey bees, is a fragrantly delicious sweetener, with a flavour profile that echoes the flowers from which it has been harvested.

For many years my father kept a couple of hives of rather ferocious bees in our city back garden. Once a year the house would be transformed to deal with his harvests – the bath rendered unusable thanks to his filtration system (which involved my mother's new nylons draped from the taps) a 44 gallon drum centrifuge occupying the laundry, and an electric drill set up in my parents' bedroom to cream bucketfuls of fresh, clear honey.

He would order his new queen bees through the mail, and I remember as a child being fascinated by the tiny boxes with little mesh windows that would arrive crashing through the letterbox onto our hall floor, their lone regal cargo quietly waiting inside her tiny prison, readied to lay thousands and thousands of eggs.

In the dry, sparse environment of Central Otago it is hard to imagine a honey bee finding anything worthy to forage, but at certain times of year the bees are kept very busy – first in early summer with the flowers of wild thyme, and later in the season with azure viper's bugloss.

My trepidation at donning a bee suit to help beekeeper Reece Adamson harvest his organic honey evaporated the moment he lifted the hive's lid. There lay honey aplenty, frame upon frame of the sweetest, palest viper's bugloss – the combined endeavour of 50,000 bees, just a single teaspoon of honey produced by each bee.

For more than 100 million years, bees have been living in colonies like this, gathering honey and pollinating plants. It is hard not to feel some sense of wonder for them and their significance in our lives – without them we would starve. But for all their outward bravado, bees are fragile creatures and right now they are in jeopardy. As guardians of our own existence we need to ensure they will survive and flourish.

Honey Lemon Cream Puddings

It's difficult to find another dessert that delivers so much for so little. Heating cream with honey and sugar then adding lemon juice creates a delicious mixture that sets to a dense, spoonable consistency. This dessert can be made up to 24 hours ahead. I like to present it in dainty antique tea cups and serve it with Slow Roasted Quinces (see below).

Prep time	6 mins + 4 hours setting time
Cook time	10 mins
Serves	6-8

600ml cream

½ cup honey

¼ cup sugar

100ml lemon juice, strained

To garnish:
fresh raspberries

Place the cream, honey and sugar in a small saucepan over a medium heat. Boil, stirring, until the sugar dissolves. Reduce the heat and simmer for 3 minutes.

Remove the saucepan from the heat and stir in the lemon juice. Strain the lemon cream through a sieve into 6-8 ramekins or cups and chill until set. This should take about 4 hours. Serve topped with fresh raspberries.

Slow Roasted Quinces

Cooking quinces very slowly at a low temperature delivers the most wonderful result. The fruit transforms to a burnished red, melting-fleshed dessert with a rich jelly.

Prep time	5 mins
Cook time	4-5 hours
Serves	6

3 whole quinces

1 cup fruity white wine such as riesling or soave, or water

3 cups sugar

Preheat oven to 150°C. Wash the quinces, rubbing any down off their skins. Cut them in half, leaving the cores in, and place them cut side down in a tightly packed single layer in a baking dish. Pour the wine or water over the top and sprinkle with the sugar.

Cover tightly and bake for 4 hours or until a rich, deep red juice has formed at the bottom of the dish.

Serve the quinces warm or chilled with a little of their jellied juices. They will keep in the fridge for several days.

Honey Vanilla Panna Cotta

Buttermilk is a low-fat alternative to the cream that is usually used in panna cotta, but you can use cream, or half cream and half milk. Don't panic if your mixture isn't getting any thicker – the gelatine won't thicken until it cools. Measure the gelatine carefully – use too much and the mixture will be rubbery. It must be added to cold water or it will go lumpy.

Prep time	20 mins
Cook time	5 mins + 3 hours chilling time
Makes	6-8

2 cups cream, divided in half

1 vanilla pod, split lengthwise, or 2 tsp vanilla extract

½ cup honey

½ cup sugar

4 tbsp cold water

4 tsp unflavoured gelatine

2 cups buttermilk

To serve:
Sunshine Fruit Topping
(see below)

Place 1 cup of the cream in a saucepan with the vanilla pod, honey and sugar and heat, stirring, until the sugar has fully dissolved. Simmer for 1 minute.

Remove the pot from the heat and lift out the vanilla pod. Split the vanilla pod open and scrape out the seeds. Add the seeds back into the cream mixture and whisk to combine (rinse the leftover pod and store it in your sugar container – it will add a nice flavour to the sugar).

Place the cold water in a small bowl and sprinkle the gelatine over the top, stirring until it is fully absorbed. Add the soaked gelatine to the hot cream, stirring until it is fully dissolved. You will know when it is dissolved because there will be no visible granules.

Cool the mixture for 15-20 minutes, stirring often (it needs to be cool before the buttermilk is added or it will split). Lightly whip the remaining cup of cream and stir it into the cooled mixture, then whisk in the buttermilk until the mixture is smooth.

Divide the mixture between 6-8 serving glasses. Cover and refrigerate until set. This should take about 3-4 hours or up to 24 hours. To serve, divide Sunshine Fruit Topping over the top of the set panna cottas. Serve chilled.

Sunshine Fruit Topping

Wash, peel and finely dice 3 peaches. Mix with the pulp of 4 passionfruit and 1 tbsp liquid honey.

Coconut Pavlovas

Pavlova is a dessert classic, but I like to add a twist by making it in individual servings. They're handy because you can cook them up to a week in advance, store them in an airtight container and add the cream and fruit topping before serving.

Prep time	15 mins
Cook time	1 hour 10 mins
Makes	6-8 individual pavlovas

6 eggs, at room temperature

a pinch of salt

1½ cups caster sugar

2 tsp cornflour

1 tsp white vinegar

1 cup coarse-thread coconut

1 tsp vanilla extract

To serve:
300ml cream, chilled

Tropical Fruit Salad
(see below)

Preheat oven to 160°C (don't use the fanbake setting). Line a baking tray with baking paper.

Make sure the bowl and beater of your food processor or electric mixer is clean and dry without a skerrick of fat. Separate the eggs and place the egg whites in the food processor or electric mixer. Add the salt and sugar and beat for about 10 minutes until shiny, glossy and very thick. Beat in the cornflour and vinegar for a few seconds, then quickly and lightly fold in the coconut and vanilla (do not beat as the oils in the coconut may deflate and soften the mixture).

Drop big spoonfuls of the mixture onto the prepared tray, making 6 to 8 individual pavlovas. The thicker you make them the more marshmallowy they will be in the middle. If you make them thinner they will be more chewy. Swirl the top into a spiral pattern with a fork or spatula. Bake for 10 minutes then turn the oven down to 130°C and bake for a further 1 hour, until the shell is crisp to the touch.

Turn off the oven and leave the pavlovas to cool in the oven for at least 2 hours. If you're not serving them the same day you can store them in an airtight container for up to a week. They can also be frozen for later use.

To serve, whip the cream until it forms soft peaks when the whisk is lifted from the bowl. Place spoonfuls of whipped cream on top of the pavlovas and spoon the Tropical Fruit Salad over the top.

Tropical Fruit Salad

Cut the skin and fibrous eyes from ½ pineapple, then remove the centre core and cut the peeled flesh into tiny batons. Peel 3 kiwifruit and cut the flesh into tiny dice. Mix together with the pineapple and the pulp from 4 passionfruit. Tropical Fruit Salad can be kept for several hours in the fridge and brought back to room temperature before serving as these fruit will not discolour.

Raspberry Cordial

Home made cordial might seem old-fashioned but it tastes much better than anything you find in a shop, plus you know exactly what's in it. Don't freak out at the amount of sugar – this recipe makes an intense concentrate that you dilute with water or soda water.

Prep time	5 mins
Cook time	10 mins
Makes	8 cups

6 cups sugar

3 cups water

grated zest of 3 unwaxed lemons

1 cup lemon juice

1 tbsp citric or tartaric acid

3 cups raspberries (fresh or frozen)

Start by thoroughly washing and sterilising several glass bottles with tight-fitting lids.

To make the base, place the sugar and water in a large saucepan and bring to a simmer, stirring until the sugar is fully dissolved. Add the lemon zest and juice to the syrup and mix in the citric or tartaric acid.

Add the raspberries, bring back to the boil and simmer for 5 minutes. Remove from the heat. Leave to cool before straining through a sieve lined with muslin, or a new J Cloth rinsed in boiling water.

Pour into the sterilised bottles, seal and store in the fridge. It will last for months. Dilute to taste with water or soda water before serving.

Elderflower Cordial

Add 40 elderflowers and 2 cups of lemon juice instead of the raspberries. Stand for 10 minutes then strain.

Currant Cordial

Add 3 cups of black or red currants instead of the raspberries and simmer for 5 minutes before straining.

Gooseberry Cordial

Add 3 cups of gooseberries instead of the raspberries and simmer for 5 minutes before straining.

Raspberry Ice Pops

Mix 1 cup Raspberry Cordial (see above) with ¼ cup water. Pour into 6 half cup ice block moulds and freeze.

Wine is the purest expression of nature, bringing us much pleasure and joy.

Something from nothing

Until lemons were introduced to the Mediterranean during the Crusades, virtually every household with access to grapes would make verjuice from the unripened grapes that were thinned before the harvest, employing the sour juice as a flavour enhancer and acid note in cooking.

The process of thinning happens at veraison, when the plant stops putting energy into leaves and starts to create sugars in the fruit. These days, the thinned grapes are usually left to go back into the ground, but it is incredibly simple to turn them into verjuice. Just blend them up, strain off the liquid and leave it for a few hours in a cold place until the sediments settle.

I was lucky enough to be at Rippon, the biodynamic vineyard of my friends the Mills family, as they were thinning the vines, so I collected a basket of unripened grapes for homemade verjuice. As verjuice ferments quickly, I froze the excess in sachets to have on hand throughout the year. Aside from the satisfaction of making something out of nothing, I have found verjuice to be an indispensable condiment that works across sweet and savoury dishes. You can equally drizzle it over sliced fruit with a sprinkle of sugar, or over oysters with a sprinkle of ground pepper.

I use verjuice to deglaze the pan after cooking meat, seafood or chicken, often adding a handful of green peppercorns or a spoonful of fruit jelly to instantly make a vibrant sauce. A splash in a tray of hot roasted vegetables or a pot of mashed potato is sensational.

Because its flavour is so mild you can use a lot more verjuice than you might lemon juice or vinegar – I like to cook a whole chicken in a couple of cups of verjuice and the pork recipe on page 159 reveals the pleasing complexity it adds. On the sweet side, it makes a lovely jelly, can be used as a spritzer with ice and soda, and is gorgeous for poaching pears and peaches.

Now I have discovered its lovely soft acidity I don't want to be without it.

Preserved Lemons

Once you see how simple it is to make this useful Fridge Fixing, you'll find yourself using Preserved Lemons in so many ways. They lend a depth of flavour to all kinds of dishes – marinades, tagines, salads, sauces, you name it! Try them in my Chermoula Marinade (see page 144) or stir them into a chicken casserole or couscous salad. Freezing the lemons first breaks down their cell structure, which speeds up the preserving process.

Prep time	15 mins
	+ freezing time
	+ pickling time
Makes	1 jar

2 lemons

2 heaped tsp salt

juice of 1 lemon

1 bay leaf

grapeseed or similar neutral oil

Scrub the lemons well and slice them lengthwise into sixths. Freeze the lemon slices on a tray until rigid.

Sterilise a medium jar and its metal lid. Take the lemons out of the freezer and pack them into the clean jar. Add the salt and lemon juice and the bay leaf. Cover with oil.

The pickled lemons will be ready in about a week but will improve over several months. Once you open the jar, you'll need to keep it in the fridge. To use the lemons, scoop out and discard the lemon flesh, then thinly slice the rinds.

Watch Annabel make this recipe at thefreerangecook.com

A good cocktail
always breaks
the ice.

Minty Mojitos

Prep time   10 mins
Serves   6

4 limes, finely chopped

2 tbsp sugar

40 mint leaves, very roughly chopped

½ cup lemon or lime cordial

1½ cups white rum

ice cubes

4 cups soda water, chilled

Roughly tumble together limes, sugar and
mint leaves to bruise mint. Add cordial and
rum and stir to combine. Fill a jug with ice,
pour in mint mixture and top up with soda.

Fisherman's Luck

Prep time   10 mins
Serves   6-8

1 bottle white wine

2 cups soda water, chilled

¾ cup Archers peach schnapps

1 peach or nectarine, very thinly sliced

1 orange, thinly sliced

1½ cups apple juice, frozen into ice cubes

Mix all the ingredients together in a large jug.
Pour into wine glasses to serve.

Watch Annabel make this recipe at thefreerangecook.com

Watermelon Cooler

Prep time	20 mins
Serves	6-8

½ large watermelon

1½ cups white rum or vodka

¾ cup fresh lime juice

To serve:
ice cubes

finely shredded mint

Cut watermelen flesh into chunks and remove seeds. Purée until smooth (yielding about 6 cups of juice). Add rum or vodka. Blend until smooth. Add lime juice and blend again. Half fill a large jug with ice and fill with watermelon mixture. Stir and garnish with mint.

Cosmopolitans

Prep time	5 mins
Serves	4

8 ice cubes

¾ cup vodka, chilled

¼ cup Triple Sec

1½ cups cranberry juice

2 tbsp fresh lime juice

To garnish:
twists of orange rind

Place ice cubes into a cocktail shaker or small jug. Add all the ingredients and stir to combine. Strain into small cocktail glasses and garnish with a twist of orange rind.

Bella's Pink Fizz

Prep time   5 mins
Serves   6

6 tbsp frozen berries such as red currants

6 tsp Berry Syrup
(see page 258)

6 tsp cassis (optional)

1 bottle Methodoise Champagne, chilled

Line up 6 champagne flutes and put 1 tbsp of frozen berries in the bottom of each glass. Drizzle 1 tsp Berry Syrup and 1 tsp cassis, if using, into each glass. Fill up carefully with bubbly and serve immediately.

Blood Orange Cocktail

Prep time   10 mins
Serves   4

4 tbsp passionfruit pulp

4 tbsp caster sugar

ice cubes

4 tbsp Campari

160ml blood orange juice

sparkling white wine or soda water, chilled

Mix passionfruit pulp with caster sugar and stir until sugar is dissolved. Half fill 4 glasses with ice. Divide passionfruit mixture between glasses. Add 1 tbsp Campari and 2 tbsp blood orange juice to each glass. Top with sparkling wine or soda, stir and serve.

Sunset Dream

Prep time   5 mins
Serves   6

2 cups ice cubes

1 cup coconut cream

2 cups pineapple juice

2 cups orange juice

a handful of mint leaves

Fill a jug with ice cubes. Add the coconut cream, pineapple juice, orange juice and mint leaves. Swirl and serve.

Summer Sangria

Prep time   5 mins
Serves   6-8

750ml bottle red wine (merlot is good)

3 cups lemonade, chilled

1 cup fresh orange juice, chilled

2-3 tbsp Grand Marnier or Cointreau

1 orange, sliced into small wedges

a handful of mint leaves

2 cups ice cubes

Mix everything together in a big jug and pour into wine glasses to serve.

Glossary

Asparagus
To cook asparagus, first remove the tough stems. Simply snap the asparagus as close as you can to the base of the stalk. It will naturally break just above the tough end. You can then trim the ends neatly before cooking. It takes just three minutes to cook in boiling water.

Baking blind
Baking blind means partially cooking an unfilled pastry shell before filling. To do this you line your baking tin with pastry, cover with baking paper then weight the paper down with uncooked rice or beans to prevent the pastry rising or collapsing at the sides. Afterwards the cooled rice or beans can be stored in an airtight jar for use again. You can also buy ceramic beans that do the same job.

Chillies
To remove seeds, cut stalk end from chilli and roll between your hands to dislodge seeds, shaking them onto the bench.

Chocolate
I like to use the best quality chocolate with 70 percent cocoa solids (such as Callebaut or Valrhona). Chocolate should be stored in a cool, dark place, not refrigerated, as it discolours with fluctuations in humidity or temperature.

Coring tomatoes
The cores of tomatoes are always tough and horrid. Use a sharp knife to cut them out.

Cutting corn from the cob
To cut the kernels from a cooked cob of corn, stand the cob upright on a chopping board and use a sharp, heavy knife in a downward motion to slice the kernels from the cob. The kernels can be frozen in a sealed vacuum bag.

Eggs
When separating eggs it's important you don't get any yolk mixed in with the whites, as this prevents the whites from foaming. Break eggs one at a time over a small bowl, passing the yolk from one half of the shell to the other while the white drips through into the bowl. Check there is no yolk in the white, before tipping it into a large, clean mixing bowl. When making meringue, use eggs that are a week or two old. Fresh whites hold together too well to fluff up. Egg whites freeze well. Thaw before using.

Espelette pepper
This is a special kind of pepper grown in the north of Spain with a distinctive smoky, sweet flavour. Substitute paprika if not available.

Garlic
If I want a fine paste texture in garlic I generally crush it by placing the peeled cloves on a board with a sprinkling of salt, and applying pressure with the flat side of a wide knife.

Ginger
Remove the skin from ginger before grating, mincing or chopping. Young ginger has a thin skin that can be scrubbed or scraped off. As it matures the skin becomes denser and needs to be peeled.

High-grade flour
This is not, as its name may suggest, a better quality flour. The name refers to this flour being high in protein, and hence gluten, which makes it a stronger flour. It should only be used in yeast cookery, rich fruit cakes and puff pastry. It produces tough, rather than tender, cakes and muffins.

Kaffir lime leaves
Before cooking remove the central rib and stem and finely chop the leaves.

Kumara

This type of sweet potato has a long history of cultivation in New Zealand. Any kind of sweet potato can be used.

Neutral oil

This can be any flavourless oil, such as grapeseed oil or rice bran oil. Use cold-pressed oils where possible.

Peppers

Peppers are also known as capsicums and bell peppers. Green capsicums are just unripe red peppers. To prepare peppers, cut in half and remove the seeds and core, then cut away and discard the white pith.

Rice

This is my fail-proof way for cooking rice. For every cup of long grain or Jasmine rice add 1½ cups cold water and ½ tsp salt. Bring to the boil, stir and cover. Reduce heat to lowest setting and cook for 12 minutes. Remove from heat and stand another 12 minutes without lifting the lid. Fluff and serve.

Sterilising jars

It is necessary to sterilise jars or bottles when preserving food. Jars and their lids must be boiled or the jars heated in an oven above 100°C to destroy all living organisms.

Fridge Fixings

You will find recipes for useful Fridge Fixings throughout this book. These handy, make-ahead sauces, dressings, flavourings and spreads can be kept on hand in the fridge or the pantry, then used as the flavour base (or starting point) for all manner of quick and easy meals.

Abbreviations

tbsp = tablespoon
tsp = teaspoon

Measures

1 tsp = 5ml
1 tbsp = 15ml
¼ cup = 60ml or 4 tbsp
½ cup = 125ml
1 cup = 250ml
4 cups = 1 litre

Oven temperatures

Unless otherwise stated all recipes in this book have been tested using the fanbake (fan forced) function. If you use regular bake you will generally need to increase the temperature by 10°C and the cook time by 10-15 percent. That said, all ovens cook differently. Use cooking times as a guide and check oven-baked items regularly. Always preheat your oven before you start cooking.

For more cooking know-how, pantry essentials and extra footage from the television series visit thefreerangecook.com

FRIDGE FIXING

Index

Thank you

There are so many wonderful people who have worked on this project, without whose skills, tireless energy and support it would never have happened. Firstly to my husband Ted, my partner in both life and in business, I wouldn't have wanted to do it without you! Throughout the demanding schedule of filming the television series and producing this book, the nourishment and hot dinners provided by you, and the support of our fabulous children Sean and Rose, have been my lifeline.

I feel tremendously lucky to work with such a talented team in my office. A big thank you to office manager Belinda Storey, publishing manager Debra Millar, designer Melissa Bulkeley, Alix Carere who photographed so many of the beautiful images in this book, copy editor Jane Binsley, food manager for the series Emerald Gilmour and Lesley Fan in the test kitchen.

Bernard Macleod and Paul Ridley at FremantleMedia Enterprises, thank you for believing in me and this idea, and giving me the wonderful opportunity to make our gorgeous television series. Thanks to the production team for the series at TVNZ, my directors, our great film crew and all the people behind the scenes. You all worked very hard, but hey, we did manage to have some fun, and even a wedding for Scott and Suzanne who met on set!

To all the people we visited to film the series and who joined us on set, generously offering time and assistance, thank you.

And finally to all my lovely friends and family, who brought me out of my tunnel for laughs and movies, walks and coffee, thanks for everything!

AN ANNABEL LANGBEIN BOOK
www.annabel-langbein.com

First published in 2010 by Annabel Langbein Media Ltd
PO Box 99068, Newmarket, Auckland 1149, New Zealand
Sixth reprint 2011

WORDS, FOOD AND STYLING Annabel Langbein
DESIGN Melissa Bulkeley
COPY EDITOR Jane Binsley
ALM PHOTOGRAPHER Alix Carere

© Recipes and text copyright Annabel Langbein 2010
© Photography copyright Annabel Langbein Media 2010,
    except where listed below.
© Design and layout copyright Annabel Langbein Media 2010

Thank you to the following photographers, who also helped make this book so beautiful, and to NZ Life & Leisure magazine, where some of the images first appeared.

© Tessa Chrisp: pg 4, 7, 8, 9, 22 (top left), 23, 42, 53 (top right), 58 & 59, 94 & 95, 138 & 139, 146 & 147, 152 (top left & below right), 198 (top & below right), 199, 214 & 215, 274 (top right), 275, 316, back cover (top left).

© Aaron McLean: pg 10, 24 (top left & below right), 31 (top left), 90 (top right), 116, 221 (centre), 223 (left & top right), 262, 269 (top left), 279 (top left), 312 (top right & left).

© Kieran Scott: pg 12, 22 (top right & below left), 31 (right), 35 (top left), 125 (top right), 198 (below left).

© Nick Tresidder: pg 280 (top left), 312 (centre left).

© Manja Wachsmuth: pg 76 (top left), 77.

ISBN 978-0-9582668-4-0
Produced by Phoenix Offset. Printed in China